D1353302

The World War II
Warship Guide

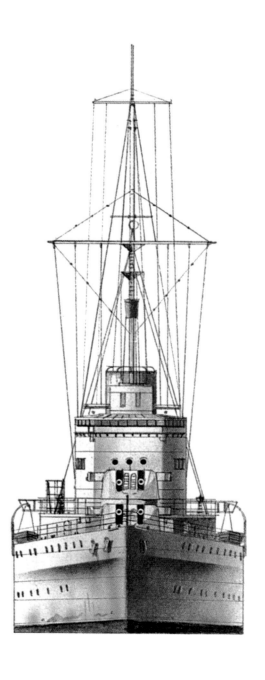

The World War II Warship Guide

Robert Hewson

20045605

MORAY COUNCIL
LIBRARIES &
INFORMATION SERVICES

623.825

Published by Silverdale Books
an imprint of Bookmart Ltd
Registered Number 2372865
Trading as Bookmart Ltd
Desford Road
Enderby
Leicester LE9 5AD

Copyright © 2000 Amber Books Ltd

All rights reserved. No part of this publication may be reproduced, stored in a retrieval system, or
transmitted in any form or by any means, electronic, mechanical, photocopying, recording or otherwise,
without the prior written permission from the publishers and the copyright holders.

ISBN 1-85605-569-8

Editorial and design by
Amber Books Ltd
Bradley's Close
74-77 White Lion Street
London N1 9PF

Project Editor: Naomi Waters
Design: Ruth Shane

Artworks courtesy of Orbis Publishing Ltd and Aerospace Publishing Ltd

Printed in Italy

Contents

Akagi

Japan's Imperial Navy was initially slow to embrace the aircraft carrier and the concept of seaborne airpower. However, as it became clear that carriers would give Japan effective striking power against the battleships of its obvious adversary, the US Navy, Japan quickly built up a carrier force that was second to none. Japanese carriers were optimised for offence – they were fast, with a substantial air wing and good AA protection – but were lightly armoured, and consequently vulnerable. One of the very first Japanese carriers was *Akagi*. This vessel was laid down as a 41,200-ton battlecruiser in 1920, but was converted to an aircraft carrier in 1923. A sister-ship, *Kaga,* followed, but it was based on a different design and *Akagi* remained unique. After its launch in 1926, *Akagi* underwent a major overhaul between 1935 and 1938, during which time the flight deck was lengthened by approximately 80ft (24.4m) from its original 624ft (190.3m). A small island was added, to port amidships, and it is in this configuration that the vessel is seen here. *Akagi* could carry up to 91 aircraft, though its normal complement was around 72, comprising 18 Aichi D1A Susie dive-bombers, 36 Yokosuka B4Y Jean torpedo-bombers and 18 Mitsubishi A5M Claude fighters. An interesting design feature was *Akagi*'s 8in (203mm) guns,

mounted on sponsons just below the flight deck, a legacy of her battlecruiser design. Another point of note was the downward-curving funnel, fitted to starboard, which replaced two smaller smoke stacks in the 1935/38 refit. *Akagi* took part in the Sino-Japanese war of 1937 but Japan's carriers' greatest hour came in the surprise attack on Pearl Harbor, on 7/8 December 1941. *Akagi* led the six carriers involved in 'Operation Z', as it was known to the Japanese high command. However, from then on Japan's hunters became the hunted, as a resurgent US Navy (led by its own carriers which had escaped the Pearl Harbor attack) launched into war across the Pacific. *Akagi* saw combat in the Pacific and Indian Oceans, where her aircraft helped sink the British cruisers *Dorsetshire* and *Cornwall,* along with the carrier HMS *Hermes.* The first major, and decisive, clash between the Japanese and US navies came at the Battle of Midway, in June 1942. During this fighting Japan lost four of its carriers, along with its most experienced naval aviators. One of those carriers was *Akagi*, sunk on 5 June 1942. The ship was wrecked by SBDs from the USS *Enterprise*, and began to burn uncontrollably. It was abandoned and sunk by accompanying Japanese destroyers.

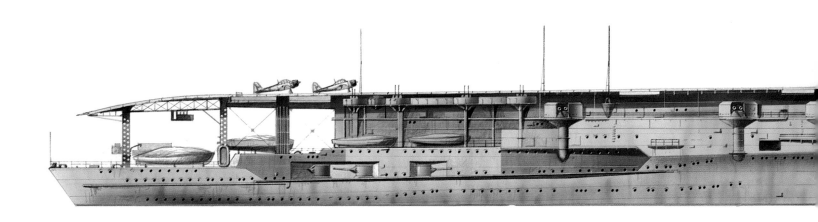

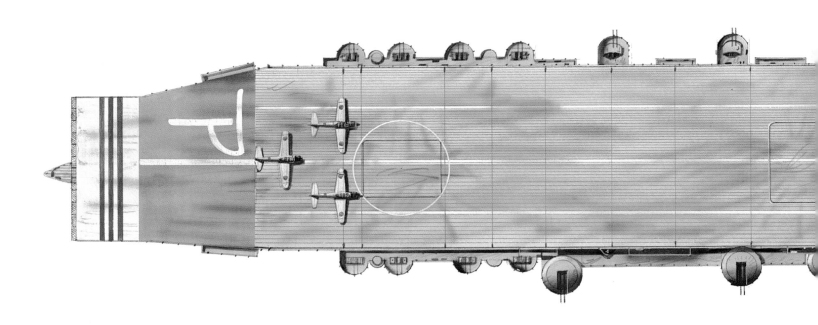

Specification

Displacement: 26,900t standard; 42,750t full load
Dimensions: length (overall) 855ft 2in (260.6m); beam (at the waterline) 102ft 9in (31.3m); draught 28ft 7in (8.71m)
Machinery: 19 Kampon boilers driving four Gijutsu-Hombu geared shaft turbines, developing 131,200hp
Maximum speed: 31kt
Armour: belt 10in (25.4cm)
Armament: 10 8in (203mm) guns, 12 4.7in (119mm) guns, 28 25mm AA guns, 60 AA machine guns, plus up to 91 aircraft
Complement: 2000
Country: Japan

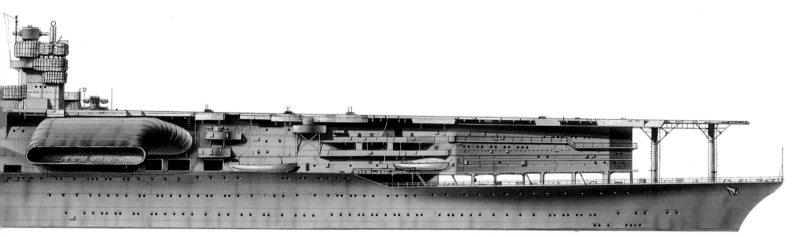

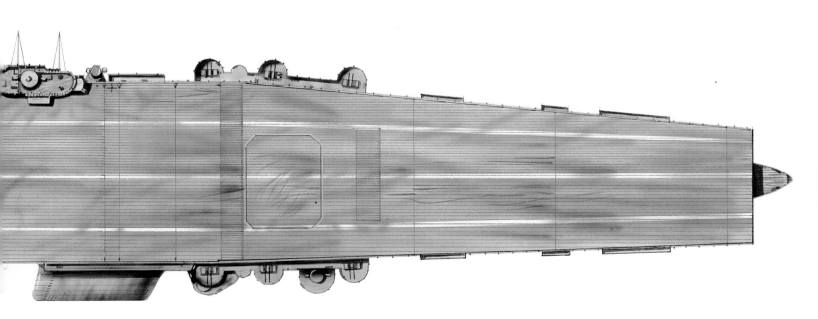

HMS *Ark Royal*

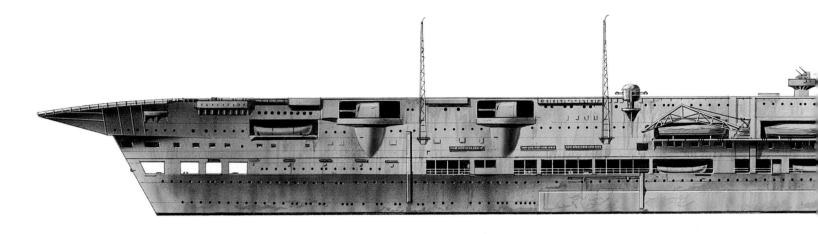

The name *Ark Royal* is the most illustrious in the Royal Navy and a succession of famous ships have carried the title. The Royal Navy's very first aircraft carrier of 1914 was named *Ark Royal*, but it was the second *Ark* that would see combat in World War II and become a household name. Britain's early experience with carrier design, and the lessons of World War I, drove the introduction of larger, well-protected carriers. These vessels protected their aircraft inside an armoured hull, using a two-storey hangar deck under the flight deck and away from the outside hull walls. The British carriers also boasted substantial defensive armament and were effective fighting ships. What they lacked, particularly in the early years of the war, were modern combat aircraft. Reliance on dated aircraft like the Fairey Swordfish severely restricted the carriers at war, though this is not to detract from the excellent record of the Swordfish in combat. When *Ark Royal* was laid down in the Cammell Laird yard in 1935 she was the largest carrier in Royal Navy history. The *Ark* was launched in 1937 and was fitted with two steam catapults. Armour protection was a priority and the vessel was built with varying layers of armour belt and underwater bulkheads to guard against surface and submarine attack. *Ark Royal* was fitted with AA guns that could fire across its own flight deck, an arrangement which – allowing for the obvious blast effects – made the guns immensely more effective for air defence. *Ark* typically carried 48 Fairey Swordfish torpedo-bombers and 24 Blackburn Skua fighter/dive-bombers. In the

early years of World War II *Ark* became a symbol of Britain's resolve and determination, as time and time again Axis propaganda claimed that she had been damaged or sunk. *Ark Royal*'s claims to fame began when one of its Skuas made the first British air-to-air kill of the war, against a German flying boat, on 26 September 1939. Acting as part of the Royal Navy's Force H, *Ark* engaged in the pursuit of the German battlecruisers *Scharnhorst* and *Gneisenau*. *Ark* and Force H were also involved in the attack on the French fleet in exile at Mers-el-Kebir, on 13 April 1940. In May 1941, Swordfish torpedo bombers, operating in appalling weather, flew repeated attacks against the *Bismarck* until finally hitting the German battleship with two torpedoes. It was the damage caused by *Ark Royal*'s aircraft that allowed other Royal Navy ships to catch the *Bismarck* and finally sink her. *Ark* was next engaged in the vital support of Malta, ferrying aircraft to the besieged island and protecting other convoys in the Mediterranean. It was on one of these missions that the carrier's luck finally ran out. While returning to Gibraltar from Malta on 13 November 1941 *Ark* was torpedoed by the German submarine *U-81*. The ship lost power and began to list alarmingly, but she was abandoned perhaps before all hope of saving her had been lost and was finally allowed to sink, 14 and a half hours after being hit – only some 25 miles (40.2km) from land on 14 November. This loss of one of the few carriers available at the time had a profound effect on subsequent British naval operations.

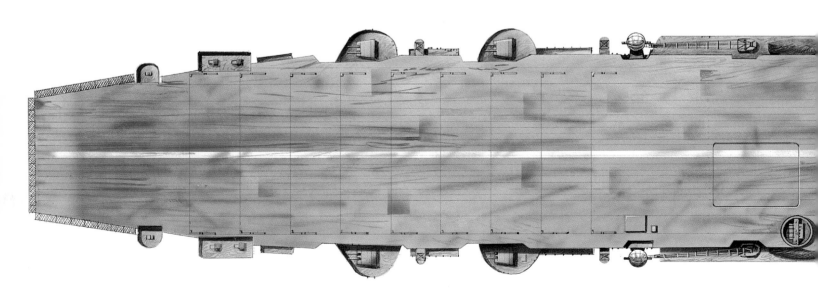

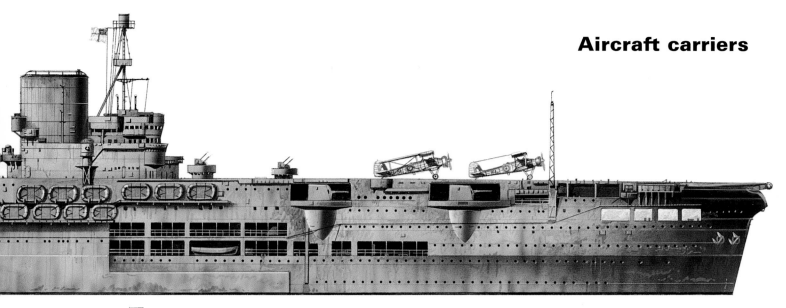

Specification

Displacement:	22,000t standard; 27,720t full load
Dimensions:	length (overall) 800ft (243.84m); beam (at the waterline) 94ft 9in (28.88m); draught 27ft 9in (8.46m)
Machinery:	six Admiralty three-drum boilers driving Parsons three-shaft geared turbines, developing 102,000hp
Maximum speed:	31kt
Armour:	belt 4.5in (11.43cm)
Armament:	16 4.5in (114mm) AA guns, 48 two-pounder 'pom pom' AA guns, plus 60 aircraft
Complement:	1580
Country:	GB

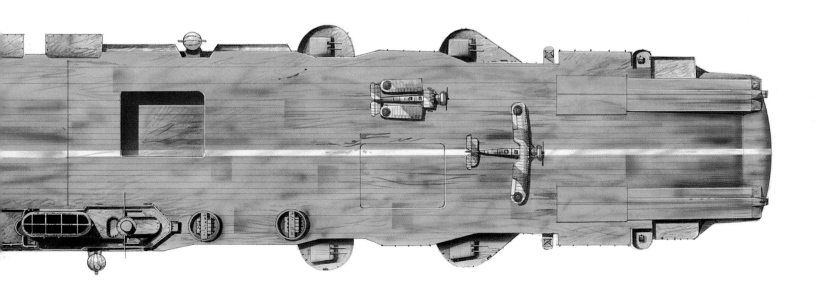

HMS *Audacity*

The escort carriers had none of the glamour or imposing size of the big carriers, but their overall role in the war was perhaps even more important. While the large carriers fought the big battles, the escort carriers spent the war years crossing the Atlantic and the Pacific, shepherding the vital convoys that were the lifeblood of the Allied war effort. With Britain so dependent on resupply from the USA, her escort carriers were of the utmost importance to provide warning and defence from German surface raiders, submarines and, in particular, long-range aircraft like the FW 200 Condor. The contribution of the escort carriers was belied by the ships themselves. Small, uncomfortable and less seaworthy then their larger siblings, many of them were converted fast cargo ships. They were lightly armed, even more lightly armoured and operated only a handful of aircraft. Nevertheless, their very presence on a convoy was a reassurance to the other ships and a deterrent to U-boats, who feared being

detected on the surface by aircraft. *Audacity* was a somewhat unusual vessel. Like most of the Royal Navy's early escort carriers, she was based on a converted cargo ship, but in this case it was the former German vessel *Hannover*, which had been captured in the West Indies in February 1940. As can be seen *Audacity* was subjected to the minimum of changes to ready her for her new role. A flight deck was added, but with no island or under-deck hangars. All of *Audacity*'s six aircraft (initially Grumman Martlets) were permanently housed above deck. The flight deck measured approximately 460ft (140.2m) x 60ft (18.29m), and had no catapults. *Audacity* was pressed into service on the Gibraltar convoys by June 1941, and became an eventual casualty, torpedoed by the *U-751* off Portugal on 21 December 1941. The carrier took three hits, breaking up and sinking 70 minutes after the first torpedo struck.

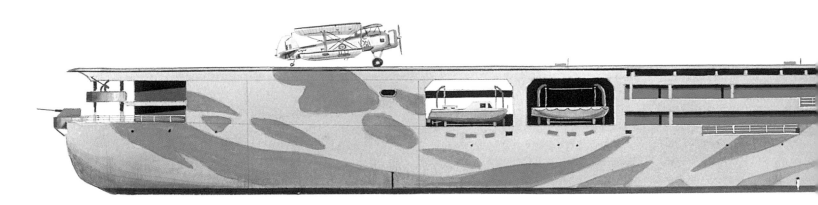

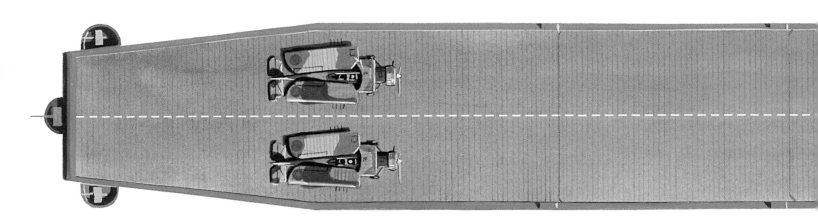

Aircraft carriers

Specification

Displacement:	11,000t deep load
Dimensions:	length (overall) 467ft 3in (145.16m); beam (at the waterline) 56ft 3in (17.14m); draught 60ft (18.29m)
Machinery:	one single-shaft diesel engine, developing 5200 hp
Maximum speed:	15kt
Armour:	none
Armament:	one 4in (102mm) gun, one six-pounder gun, four two-pounder 'pom pom' AA guns, four 20mm AA guns, plus six aircraft
Complement:	not known
Country:	GB

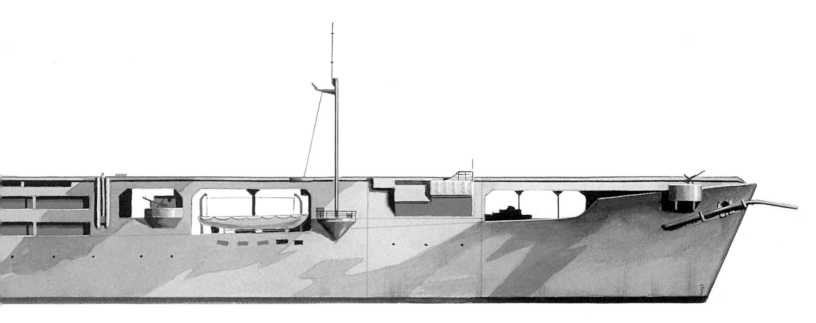

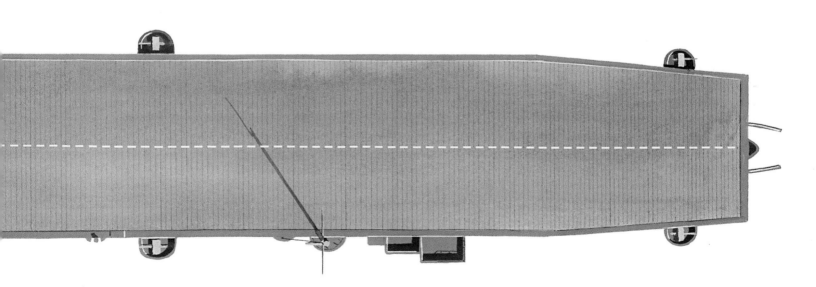

USS *Independence* (CVL-22)

The USS *Independence* or 'Indy', as she was known to her crews, was the lead ship in the *Independence*-class of light aircraft carriers (CVLs), built as a stop-gap measure for the US Navy soon after America's entry into the war. By early 1942 the USN had a programme in place to build the *Essex* class of fast carriers (CVs), but it was feared that these ships would not be available soon enough. In the event, these fears proved unfounded, as the United States' massive industrial capabilities swung behind a frenzy of ship-building. The *Essex*-class carriers went on to become the mainstay of the US Fast Carrier Task Forces throughout the war, but they were joined by the nine CVLs of the *Independence* class. *Indy* and her sister-ships were all based on *Cleveland*-class cruisers, and converting these narrow hulls into carriers was no easy task. The nine light carriers were built at the New York Ship Builders yards, where they were laid down between 1941 and 1942. All were launched by 1943. *Independence* was the former USS *Amsterdam* (CL-59), and was laid down on 1 June 1941. As CVL-22, she was launched on 22 August 1942 and commissioned on 1 January 1943. Their cruiser origins meant that the CVLs displaced about a third as much tonnage as a regular fleet carrier and could carry only half the air wing of a CV – comprising 12 F6F Hellcats, nine SBD Dauntless and nine TBM Avengers by 1942. The USS *Independence* was fitted with twin 5in (127mm) gun mounts fore and aft, the only one of the class to be so armed. *Indy* (and the second CVL USS *Princeton*) was also built without any side armour, so hurried was her construction.

All but one of the CVLs *(Princeton)* survived the war. Though they had successful operational careers, they were small, slow and far from modern in design. *Independence* was hit by a Japanese aerial torpedo which put it out of action from November 1943 until mid-1944. Following this she saw uninterrupted service until VJ-Day. After the surrender of Japan the *Independence*-class CVLs were all quickly taken out of service and largely broken up or sold abroad. The USS *Independence* was one of the target ships used in the Crossroads nuclear tests at Bikini Atoll in 1946, but she survived largely undamaged. *Indy* was ultimately 'expended' (sunk) in weapons tests on 29 January 1951. The *Independence* name was later allocated to the last of the US Navy's *Forrestal*-class carriers, commissioned in 1959. As CV 62, the 'new' USS *Independence* served until she was in turn decommissioned in 1998.

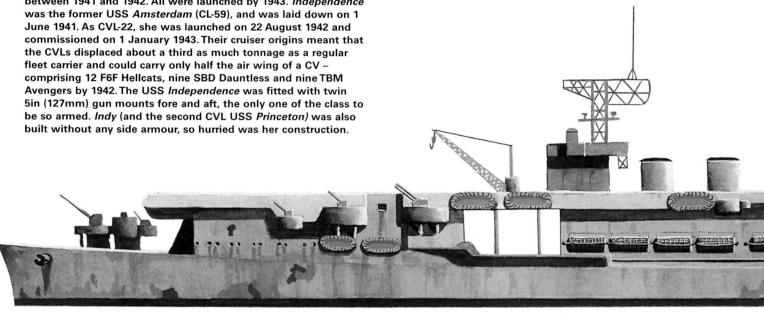

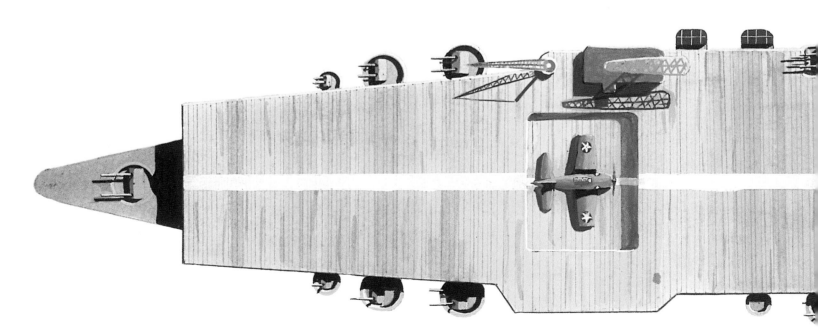

Aircraft carriers

Specification

Displacement: 10,662t standard; 14,751t deep load
Dimensions: length (overall) 622ft 6in (189.97m); beam (at the waterline) 71ft 6in (21.8m); draught 24ft 3in (7.39m)
Machinery: four Babcock and Wilcox boilers driving four-shaft General Electric turbines, developing 100,000hp
Maximum speed: 31.6kt
Armour: belt 5in (12.7cm); bulkheads 5in/1.5in (12.7/3.81cm); armoured deck over belt 2in (5.08cm) (no armour belt on CV 22)
Armament: (by 1945) 28 40mm AA guns, four 20mm AA guns (CV 22 only), plus 30 aircraft (standard)
Complement: 1569
Country: USA

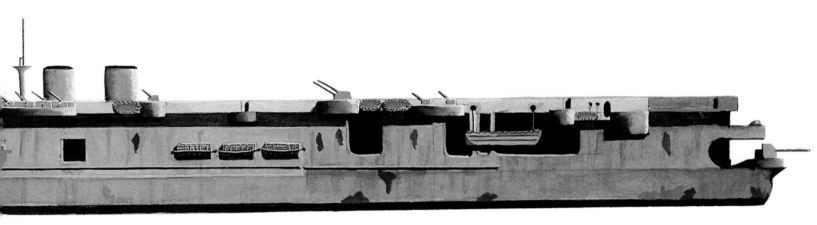

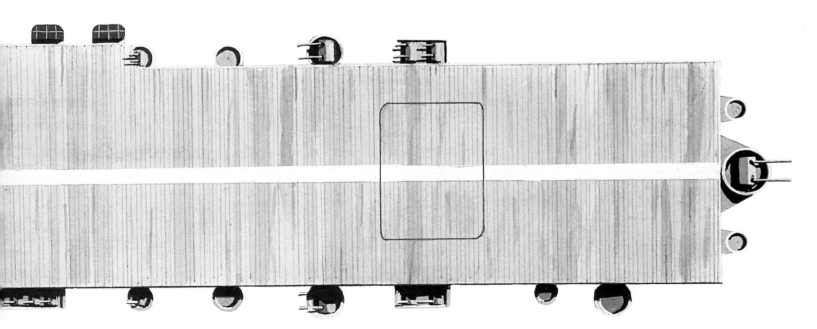

HMS *Indomitable*

HMS *Indomitable* was one of the modest number of modern fleet aircraft carriers available to the Royal Navy in the early years of World War II. It was originally intended to be the fourth in the *Illustrious* class (after *Illustrious*, *Victorious* and *Formidable*) but, in the event, *Indomitable* had marked differences to its predecessors. The British philosophy of aircraft carrier design championed heavily-armoured vessels that could withstand attacks from naval gunfire as well as enemy aircraft. This armour protection came at a price: that of reduced aircraft capacity. The large *Illustrious*-class carriers had a complement of just 36 aircraft. When *Indomitable* took shape at the Vickers-Armstrong shipyard in Barrow, its armour-plated belt was reduced by 3in (76mm), allowing it to accommodate larger hangars and thus more aircraft. *Indomitable* was laid down on 10 November 1937, launched on 26 March 1940 and commissioned into Royal Navy service on 10 October 1941. Her flight deck initially measured 680ft x 95ft (207.3m x 28.95m), but was later lengthened to 745ft (227m). The deck was also raised by 14ft (4.27m) to permit the addition of a second hangar. In this configuration *Indomitable*

could carry up to 56 aircraft. The vessel's armament was also revised several times, as more and more defensive guns were added throughout the course of the war. *Indomitable* had an eventful wartime career and saw much action. The ship was attacked and damaged on several occasions and put out of service twice by enemy action. On 12 August 1942, during Operation Pedestal, she suffered two direct hits and three near-misses from bombs that disabled the ship and forced her out of service for six months. After her return to service, a torpedo attack on 16 July 1943 holed the ship and caused severe flooding. *Indomitable* heeled over 12.5° in the water, but calm seas and effective action by the crew prevented her loss. *Indomitable* was out of service after this attack for 34 weeks. After repair in the USA, she joined the British forces in the Pacific in July 1944. On 4 May 1945 *Indomitable* was hit by a Japanese kamikaze attack but went on to see out the end of the war safely. After post-war service in the Mediterranean and Home Fleets, *Indomitable* was eventually withdrawn from service and broken up in 1955.

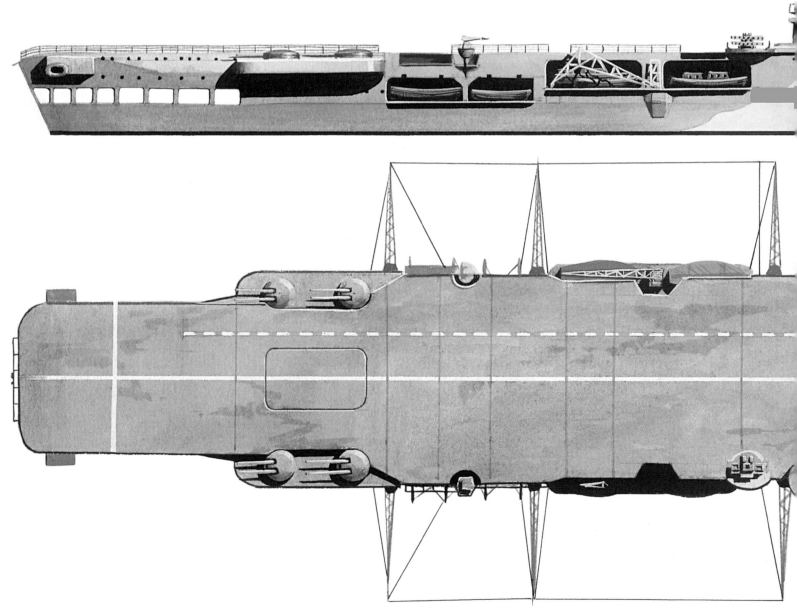

Specification

Displacement:	23,000t standard; 29,730t deep load
Dimensions:	length (overall) 753ft 11in (229.8m); beam (at the waterline) 95ft 9in (29.18m); draught 29ft (8.84m)
Machinery:	six Admiralty three-drum boilers driving three-shaft Parsons geared turbines, developing 111,000hp
Maximum speed:	30.5kt
Armour:	belt 4.5in (114mm); hangar side 1.5in (38mm); bulkheads 3 in/1.5 in (76mm/38mm); flight deck 3in (76mm)
Armament:	(by 1945) 16 4.5in (114mm) guns, 48 two-pounder 'pom pom' AA guns, 12 40mm twin Bofors AA guns, 13 40mm single Bofors AA guns, 36 20mm Oerlikon AA guns plus 45 aircraft (standard)
Complement:	1392 initially, 2100 later
Country:	GB

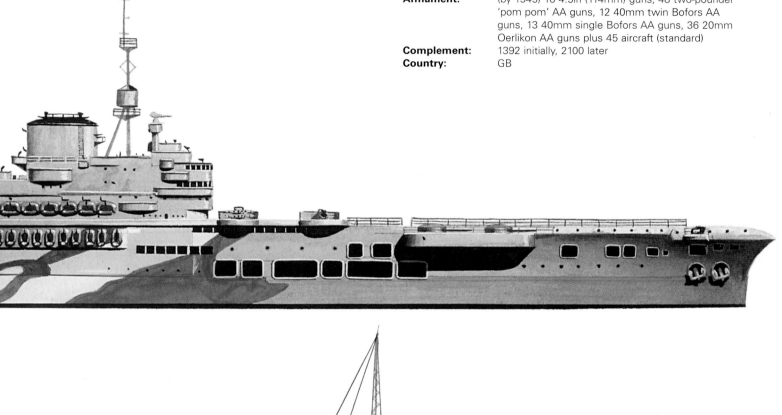

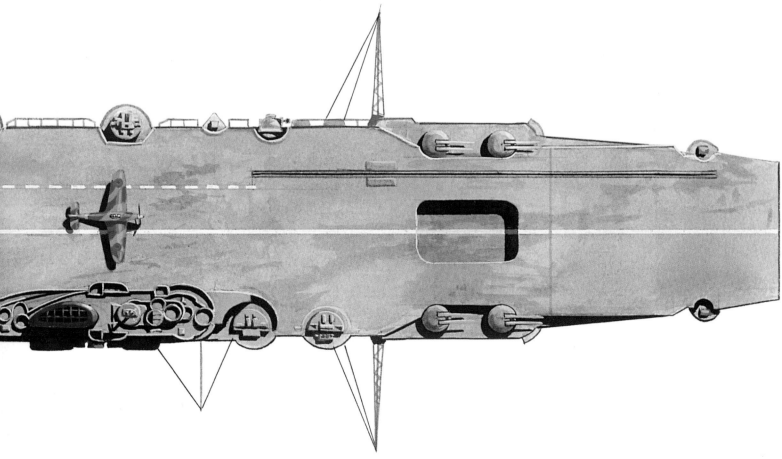

Kaga

Like the *Akagi*, Japan's *Kaga* was born in the aftermath of the 1922 Washington Naval Disarmament Treaty, an international arms limitation agreement that capped Japan's naval forces at a level far short of its ambitions. At that time Japan had embarked on its '8-8' plan to build eight modern battleships and eight cruisers. This was blocked by the Washington Treaty but it did allow Japan to convert some of the hulls it had already started work on, into aircraft carriers. *Kaga* was laid down as a 40,000-ton battleship and, despite its unsuitability to the task, the order was given to convert it into a carrier. Work began on *Akagi* and *Kaga* at the same time and the two have often been referred to as sister-ships. In fact, while the conversion process was similar, there were several important differences between the vessels. *Kaga* was laid down in 19 July 1920, launched on 17 November 1921 and commissioned on 31 March 1928, though the vessel did not enter fully active service until 1934. Then, *Kaga* underwent the same process of modification and modernisation as *Akagi*. The flight deck was extended to cover the complete length of the hull, additional hangarage was added to boost the number of

embarked aircraft to 72 (with up to 18 possible additional reserves), a third deck lift was added, new boilers and turbines were fitted, armament was completely revised and an island was constructed, forward of amidships and to starboard. *Kaga's* earlier funnel, which ran half the length of the ship to discharge at the stern, was replaced by a neater, downwards-pointing unit. *Kaga* was designed to carry 24 Aichi D1A Susie dive-bombers, 36 Yokosuka B4Y Jean torpedo-bombers and 12 Mitsubishi A5M Claude fighters but, with the introduction of the larger Nakajima B5N Kate torpedo-bomber in 1938, the air group decreased to 66 aircraft. *Kaga's* aircraft played a pivotal role in the Shanghai Incident of 1932 and the vessel was active throughout the Sino-Japanese fighting in 1939. *Kaga* participated in the attack on Pearl Harbor and later in the February 1942 raids on Darwin, Australia, and the invasion of Rabul in March 1942, as did *Akagi*. Also like *Akagi*, *Kaga* met her fate at the Battle of Midway, when she was hit by dive-bombers from the USS *Enterprise*, set on fire and finally exploded, sinking on 4 June 1942.

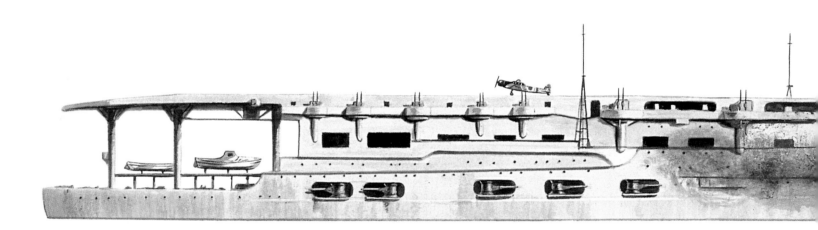

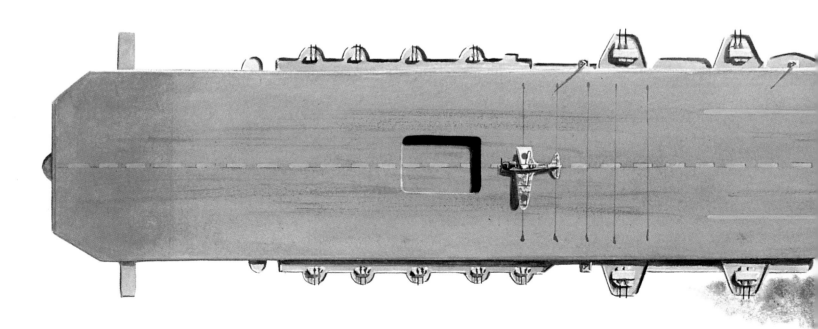

Specification

Displacement:	38,200t standard; 43,650t full load
Dimensions:	length (overall) 812ft 6in (247.65m); beam (at the waterline) 106ft 7in (32.48m); draught 31ft 1in (9.47m)
Machinery:	12 Kampon boilers driving four Brown-Curtis turbines, developing 91,000hp
Maximum speed:	27.5kt
Armour:	belt 11in (280mm)
Armament:	10 8in (203mm) guns, 16 5in (127mm) guns, 22 25mm AA guns, 60 AA machine guns plus up to 91 aircraft
Complement:	2016
Country:	Japan

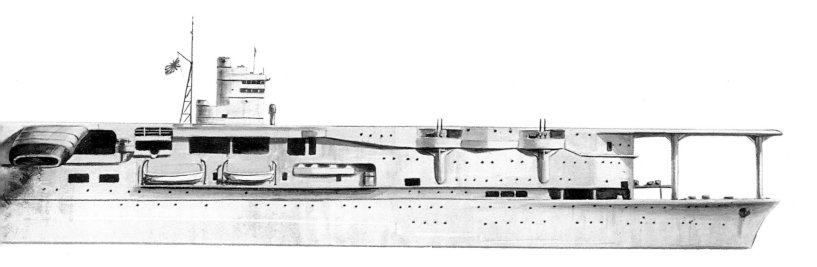

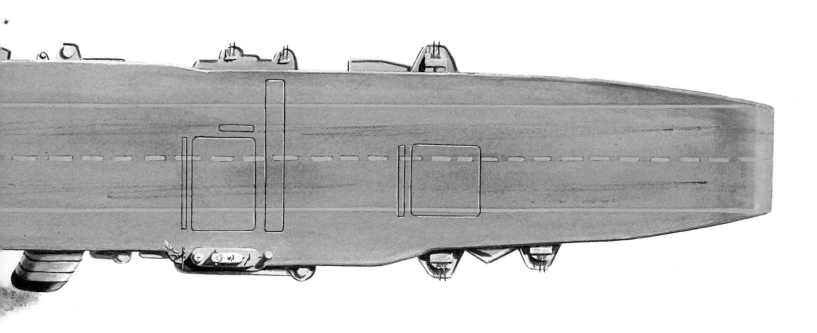

USS *Lexington* (CV-2)

The two ships of the *Lexington* class – USS *Lexington* (CV-2) and USS *Saratoga* (CV-3) – were the United States' first effective aircraft carriers. They were also the largest, most heavily-armed and best-protected of their peers. This was due to their origins, like so many other carriers of that period, in the 1922 Washington Treaty. The *Yorktown* class were designed as 43,000-ton battlecruisers which the US Navy speedily converted to carrier status when its battleship/cruiser-building programme was cut back by the Washington Treaty. As a result, *Lexington* went on to become an aircraft carrier that possessed battleship armament and cruiser armour. Its size and weight called for equally substantial powerplants and the *Lexington*s would hold the distinction of being the world's most powerful warships right up to the end of World War II. A graphic illustration of this came in 1929-30, when *Lexington*'s generators provided power for the entire city of Tacoma, Washington, after the local hydro-electric powerplant failed in the middle of winter. *Lexington* was laid down on 8 January 1921, launched on 3 October 1925 and commissioned on 14 December 1927. She was designed to carry 80 of the US Navy's first-generation carrier-borne aircraft (F6C, FB, OU and T3M). *Lexington*'s substantial hangar space would become a boon in later years when larger aircraft were

introduced. *Lexington* had a massive funnel, 80ft (24.38m) high, housing four smoke stacks. Forward of this was the bridge superstructure (it was not really an island) and both the bridge and funnel were flanked by eight Mk 14 8in (375mm) guns. These guns were a throwback to *'Lady Lex's'* cruiser design, but they were an ultimately pointless addition to the ship as a carrier. Realistically, they could only fire in one direction and in a limited arc. *Saratoga* had her gun installation changed, but *Lexington* never did. Indeed, most of the modifications and new equipment applied to *Saratoga* never made it on to the *Lexington*, but like all wartime carriers *Lexington* was progressively up-gunned to meet the threat of enemy aircraft. *Lexington* and *Saratoga* carried all of the US Navy's biplane and early monoplane combat aircraft and, by the end of the war, *Saratoga* was operating 70

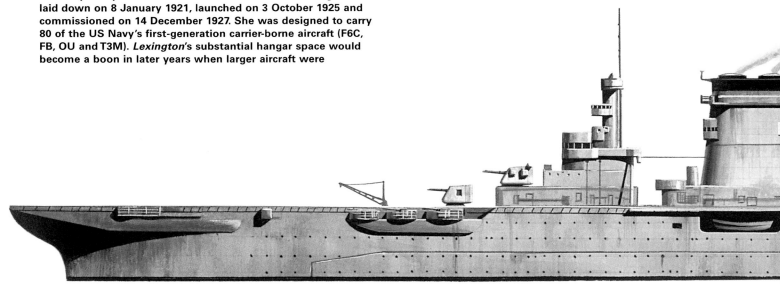

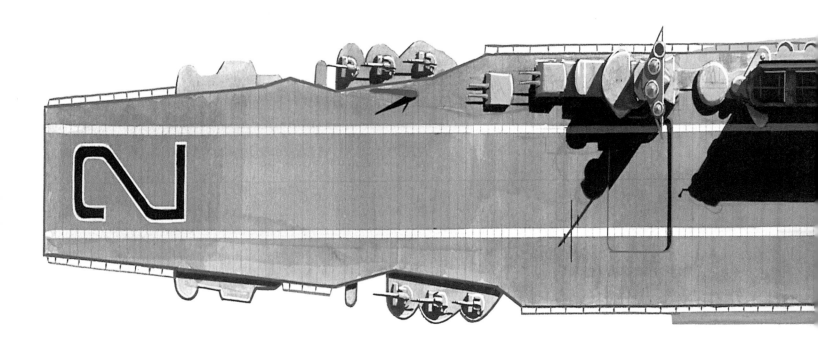

F6F Hellcats and TBM Avengers. However, *Lexington* did not make it that far. Her war began soon after the Pearl Harbor attack with skirmishes against Japanese units off Rabul and New Guinea. Acting as part of Task Force 11, *Lexington* was heavily involved in the fighting off Bougainville, in the Solomons, in February 1942. It was during this campaign that Lt Edward 'Butch' O'Hare, flying from the *Lex,* became the first US Navy ace of World War II. On 10 March *Lexington* launched a surprise attack against Japanese targets around the Gulf of Papua, at Salamaua and Lae. On 8 May 1942, she was attacked by aircraft from *Shokaku* and *Zuikaku,* suffering serious damage from bombs and torpedoes. Badly damaged and on fire, *Lexington* was scuttled, and sunk by torpedoes fired by the destroyer USS *Phelps*.

Specification

Displacement:	37, 681t standard; 43,055t full load
Dimensions:	length (overall) 888ft (270.66m); beam (at the waterline) 105ft 5in (32.13m); draught 33ft 4in (10.16m)
Machinery:	16 Yarrow boilers, driving four-shaft General Electric turbines, developing 180,000hp
Maximum speed:	33.25kt
Armour:	belt 5in to 7in (127mm to 178mm); flight deck 1.25in (32mm)
Armament:	eight 8in (203mm) guns (later removed), 12 5in (127mm) guns, 48 .5in (12.7mm) machine guns, plus 63 aircraft (standard)
Complement:	2327
Country:	USA

USS *Sangamon* (CVE-26)

During World War II the United States built a mass of light and escort carriers to fill the endless demand for shipborne airpower. The escort carriers had an essential role in protecting convoys, though as the threat to the convoys diminished they were redeployed on more active combat roles. The US Navy escort carriers generally spent less time on convoy duties than their Royal Navy counterparts (particularly in the Atlantic). The *Sangamon*-class ships were escort carriers, pressed into service by the US Navy in 1942. Most of the initial batches of escort carriers were hastily converted C3 cargo ships, but the *Sangamons* were built on T3 tanker hulls. Tankers (oilers) were in desperately short supply themselves, and the fact that four were turned into aircraft carriers highlights the overriding importance of air power at that time. Like the other ships in her class (USS *Suwannee*, USS *Chenango* and USS *Santee*) the USS *Sangamon* had a longer flight deck and more hangar space than her contemporaries (thanks to her different basic design). The *Sangamons* were also faster than other escort carriers, though they were essentially unarmoured and retained large openings amidships, allowing them to function as oilers if required. The flight deck had two lifts and a single catapult, positioned to port.

The lattice mast above the island was an SC radar. USS *Sangamon* could carry up to 35 aircraft, but the usual complement was 30. A standard air wing included F4F Wildcats or F6F Hellcats and TBF Avengers. The *Sangamons* were the only escort carriers to (sometimes) carry SBD Dauntless dive-bombers. USS *Sangamon* was used to conduct early deck trials of the Vought F4U Corsair (as seen here) but these proved unsuccessful and so the illustrious Corsair was actually kept off the flight deck of any US carrier until December 1944. USS *Sangamon* was laid down on 13 March 1939, launched on 4 November 1939 and commissioned on 25 August 1942. Her three sister-ships were all in service by September. *Sangamon* entered service just in time to support the Operation Torch landings in North Africa in 1942, and spent the rest of her wartime career in the Pacific theatre. *Sangamon* served as an attack carrier and later a transport and training ship. She was hit by Japanese bombs and a kamikaze attack in 1944 and suffered a second kamikaze attack in April 1945. The damage was never really repaired. USS *Sangamon* was struck off the Navy's active list soon after the war ended, and finally broken up in 1948.

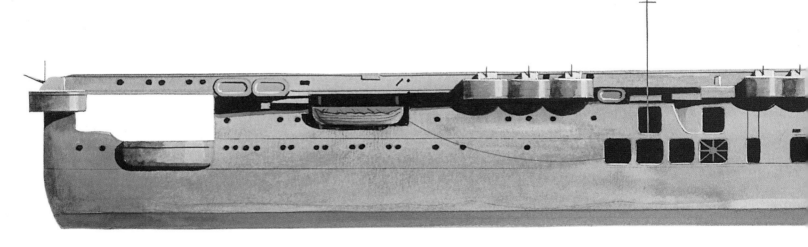

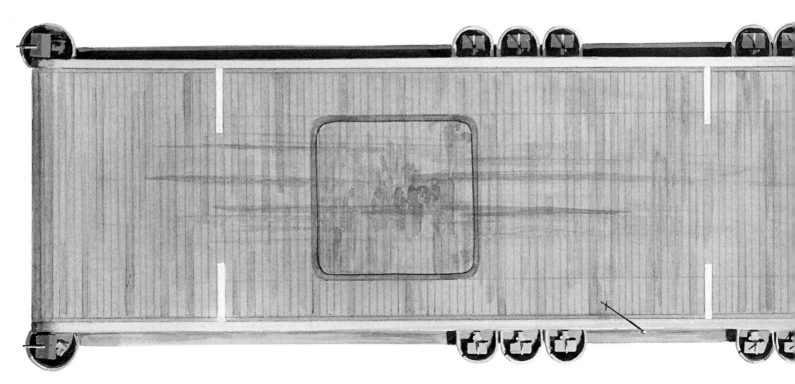

Aircraft carriers

Specification

Displacement: 10,494t standard; 23,875t full load
Dimensions: length (overall) 553ft (168.55m); beam (at the waterline) 75ft (22.86m); draught 30ft 7in (9.32m)
Machinery: four Babcock and Wilcox boilers, driving two-shaft General Electric turbines, developing 13,500hp
Maximum speed: 18kt
Armour: none
Armament: two 5in (127mm) guns, eight 40mm AA guns, 12 20mm AA guns, plus 30 aircraft
Complement: 1080
Country: USA

Shinano

Had she made it into active service, *Shinano* would have immediately become the largest carrier ever in the Japanese Imperial Fleet, and the largest of the war. Not until the arrival of the nuclear-powered USS *Enterprise* (CVN-65) did a bigger carrier take to the seas. The early carrier battles of the war quickly taught the Japanese navy that the aircraft carrier could negate any and every battleship, and so everything possible had to be done to maximise the number of carriers available (especially after the losses at Midway). By mid-1942 Japan had three of the mighty *Yamato*-class battleships under construction, but the third vessel was then still only a hull. Work on the battleship *Shinano* ceased and the vessel instead became a large carrier which retained the armour protection of a battleship along with a huge capacity for aircraft and fuel. The intended armour belt of 15.7in (39.88cm) was reduced to 8.1in (20.57cm), except along the magazines, but this was still a level of

protection higher than any other carrier – even the flight deck had over 3in (76mm) of armour. Because of *Shinano*'s great size it was planned that she would serve as a unique resupply carrier for the rest of the fleet. *Shinano* could embark up to 50 aircraft of her own, but in addition to that she would carry yet more aircraft, fuel and supplies that could be flown out to replenish other carriers. In this way Japan's carriers would have less need to return to port and could stay operational for longer. *Shinano* was laid down on 4 May 1940 and launched on 8 October 1944; however, the Japanese navy never got the chance to try out its new tactic. While being moved to Kure for final fitting out, *Shinano* was torpedoed four times by the submarine USS *Archerfish* on 29 November 1944. The ship had no damage control teams or equipment, and flooding could not be contained. Despite this, it took seven hours for *Shinano* to sink, a tribute to its well-protected construction.

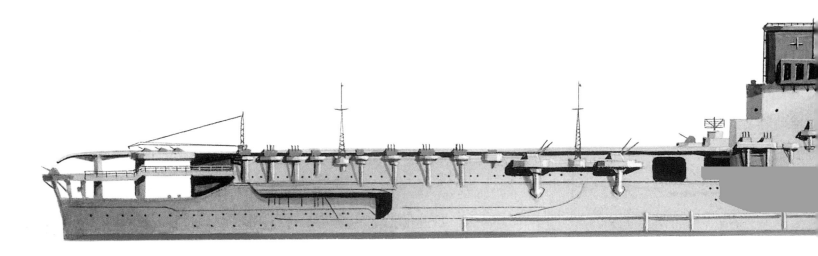

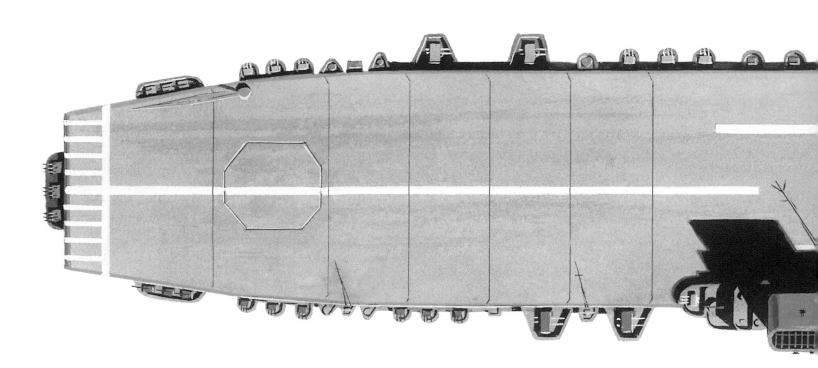

Aircraft carriers

Specification
Displacement: 62,000t standard; 71,890t full load
Dimensions: length (overall) 872ft 8in (265.98m); beam (at the waterline) 119ft 1in (36.29m); draught 33ft 10in (10.31m)
Machinery: 12 Kampon boilers, driving Kampon four-shaft geared turbines, developing 150,000hp
Maximum speed: 27kt
Armour: belt 8.1in (205mm); flight deck 3.1in (78mm); hangar deck 7.5in (190mm)
Armament: 16 5in (127mm) guns, 145 25mm AA guns, 12 28-barrelled rocket launchers, plus 47 aircraft (standard)
Complement: 2400
Country: Japan

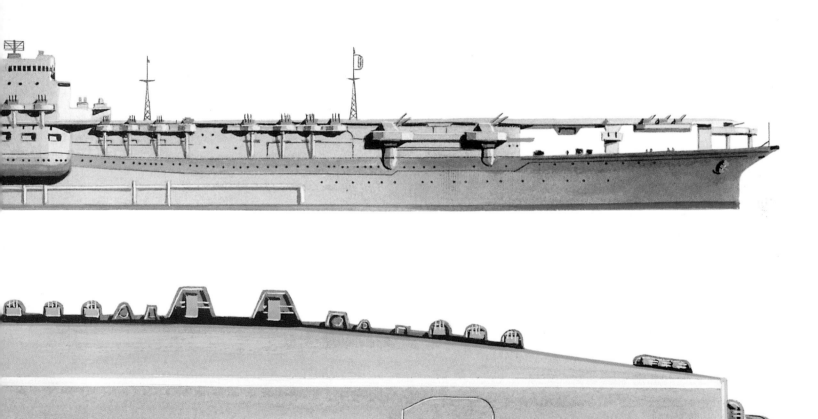

Taiho

Taiho and her planned sisterships represented a major step forward in Japanese carrier design, but by the time Taiho was launched Japan was already on the back foot in the Pacific, and new carriers could not stem the tide of the war. Taiho was Japan's largest and most modern aircraft carrier of World War II and introduced several design features not seen on Japanese ships before. These included an armoured flight deck, protected by 3in (76mm) plate which could survive a hit from a 1,000lb (453kg) bomb in some circumstances. Taiho's flight deck was also longer than any other carrier in the Imperial Navy. In some respects the thinking behind her design reflected the British approach, as Taiho incorporated long two-storey armoured

aircraft hangars. These hangars were well-protected above and below but not at the sides, and so they lacked the fully-protected 'box' of vessels like HMS Illustrious. Taiho's hull was armour plated right up to the flight deck – another unique Japanese feature that was common on British carriers. Taiho was laid down on 10 July 1941, launched on 7 April 1943 and commissioned on 7 March 1944. The ship's official air wing was posted at 60 aircraft, though it had the hangar space to carry up to 75. Within a few weeks of her first shake down cruise Taiho was sunk during the Battle of the Philippine Sea. On 19 June 1944 she was torpedoed by the submarine Albacore and was destroyed in a massive explosion – caused by fuel vapour – a few hours later.

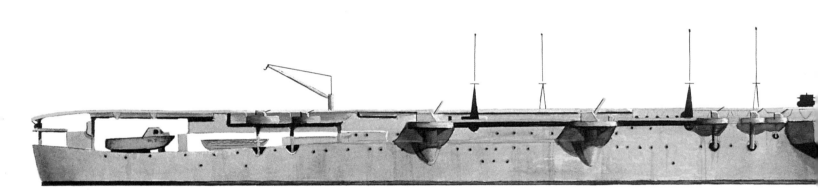

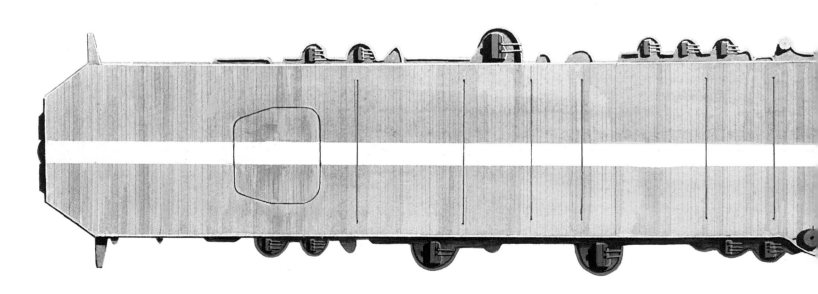

Aircraft carriers

Specification

Displacement:	29,300t standard; 37,270t deep load
Dimensions:	length (overall) 855ft (260m); beam (at the waterline) 98ft 6in (30m); draught 31ft 6in (9.6m)
Machinery:	eight Kampon boilers, driving geared turbines, developing 160,000hp
Maximum speed:	33kt
Armour:	belt 2.2in (machinery), 5.9in (150mm) (magazines), flight deck 3.1in (77mm), lower hangar deck 4.9in (124mm)
Armament:	12 100mm (3.9in) guns, 71 25mm AA guns plus 60 aircraft (standard)
Complement:	1751
Country:	Japan

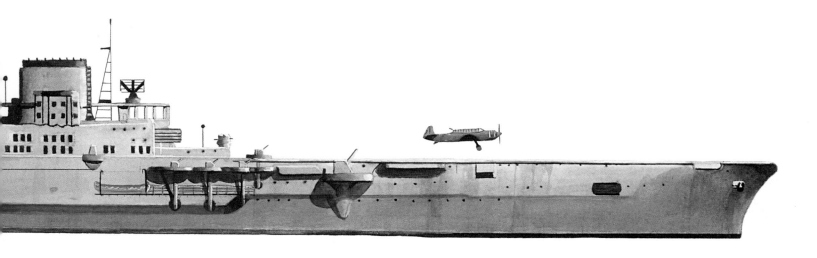

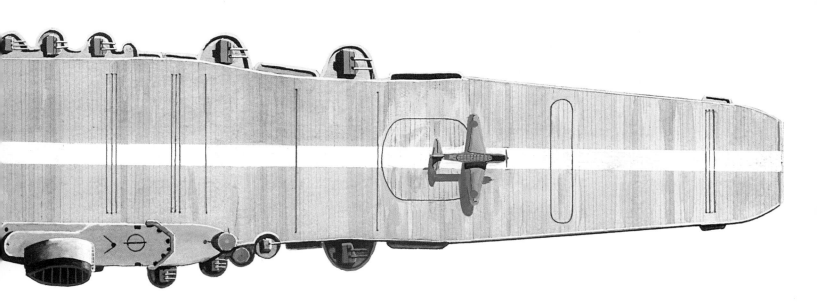

USS *Wasp* (CV-7)

The USS *Wasp* was a vessel which arguably should never have been built. She was a product of the 1922 Washington Treaty, which limited the total tonnage allowed to each of the world's major navies. After the US Navy had laid down the carriers USS *Yorktown* and *Enterprise*, in 1934, it still had 15,000 tons unbuilt under the terms of the Treaty. The USS *Wasp* was conceived to 'soak up' this available tonnage, but it was demanded that *Wasp* incorporate as many features of the *Yorktown* class as possible. The result was an awkward compromise. *Wasp* was a much smaller ship (15,000 tons compared to 20,000 tons), so to accommodate the required number of aircraft, her machinery was drastically cut back and armour-protection was left at a minimum. There were plans to improve *Wasp's* level of protection once she was in service – in particular to give her effective anti-torpedo armouring – but this never went ahead. Plans also existed to give *Wasp* a second flight deck by allowing aircraft to fly off from the hangar deck, but the available space was soon filled up with the catapult mechanisms. The space under the

flight deck was left open, though it could be closed off in bad weather. *Wasp* was laid down on 1 April 1936, launched on 4 April 1939 and commissioned on 25 April 1940. Her initial air group comprised four squadrons: one fighter, one dive-bomber and two scout-bomber units. *Wasp* had no provision for torpedo storage so she did not carry torpedo-bombers until August 1942. These were the TBF Avengers of VT-7, which came aboard just a few weeks before the carrier was sunk. *Wasp* entered the war serving with the US Atlantic Fleet. In 1942 she played a vital role in the relief of Malta: between March and May 1942 *Wasp* made two trips to the island to deliver 100 Spitfires. After this, *Wasp* was dispatched to the Pacific to aid the attacks on Guadalcanal in June 1942. It was during this period that *Wasp* was torpedoed by the Japanese submarine *I-19* on 15 September 1942. On fire, the carrier was abandoned and sunk by more torpedoes, fired from the destroyer USS *Lansdowne*. *Wasp's* lack of underwater protection had proved to be her undoing.

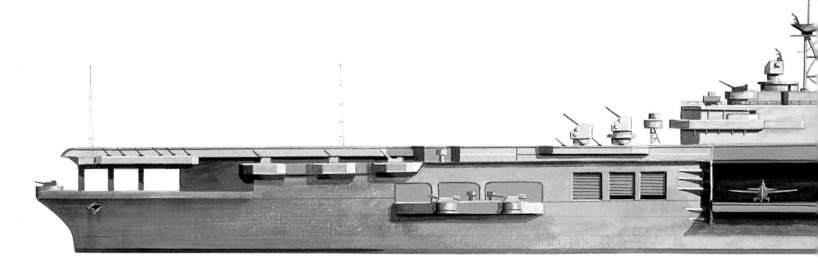

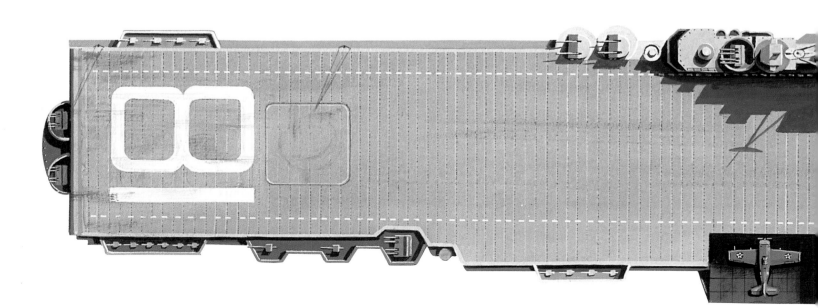

Specification

Displacement:	14,700t standard; 18,450t full load
Dimensions:	length (overall) 720ft (219.45m); beam (at the waterline) 81ft 7in (24.86m); draught 23ft 3in (7.1m)
Machinery:	six Yarrow boilers, driving Parsons two-shaft turbines, developing 70,000hp
Maximum speed:	29.5kt
Armour:	belt 0.625in (16mm); flight deck 1.25in (31mm)
Armament:	eight 5in (127mm) guns, 16 28mm guns, 25 12.7mm machine gun launchers, plus 76 aircraft (standard)
Complement:	2167
Country:	USA

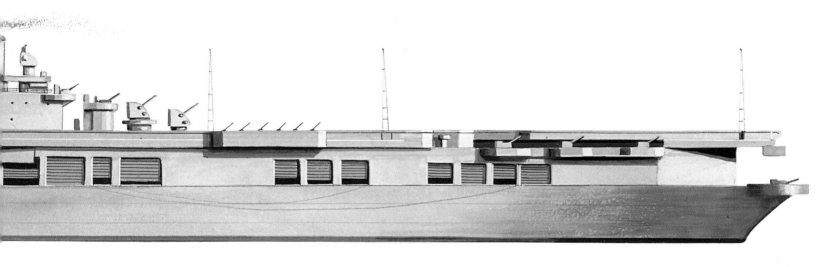

USS *Yorktown* (CV-5)

As the lead ship of her class, the USS *Yorktown* became the first truly modern carrier to enter US Navy service in the pre-World War II years. Along with her sister-ships – the USS *Enterprise* (CV-6) and the USS *Hornet* (CV-8), which was built four years after the first two – *Yorktown* also became one of the most illustrious American carriers. From the outset, the *Yorktown*s were designed to be big ships, the biggest allowed under Washington Treaty limitations. *Yorktown*'s aircraft hangars were built as lightweight superstructure, with open sides. This allowed aircraft to warm up their engines before launch but not fill the area with fumes. It also allowed *Yorktown* to be more easily fuelled and replenished at sea. Neither the hangars nor flightdeck were armoured: the deck was made from wood. *Yorktown* was fitted with two main catapults on the forward flight deck, and three aircraft deck lifts. She was laid down on 21 May 1934,

1937. The basic design called for the ship to accommodate 18 F2Fs, 36 TBDs and 37 BTs or SBCs (plus another five aircraft), but *Yorktown* rarely went to sea with more than 80 aircraft. New radar and more AA guns were added by 1942, when *Yorktown* was transferred to the Pacific. Early that year her aircraft were active, attacking Japanese targets on and around New Guinea. Then in May, *Yorktown*'s air wing participated in the sinking of the Japanese carrier *Shoho* and damaged *Shokaku* at Coral Sea. *Yorktown* was damaged during this action, but was repaired in time for the Battle of Midway. On 4 June 1942, *Yorktown*'s aircraft put the carrier *Soryu* out of the war, but then *Yorktown* herself was heavily attacked and crippled by Japanese aircraft. Badly damaged and under tow, *Yorktown* was torpedoed by the Japanese submarine *I-168* two days later, and sank on the following day, 7 June 1942.

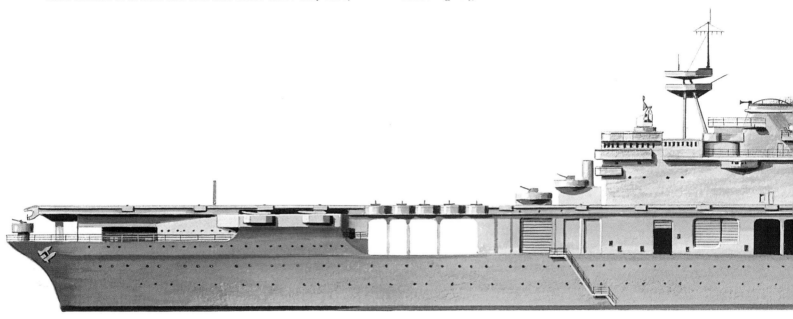

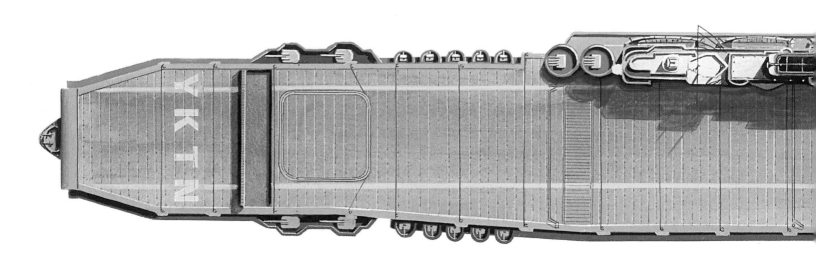

Aircraft carriers

Specification

Displacement:	19,875t standard; 25,484t full load
Dimensions:	length (overall) 809ft (246.6m); beam (at the waterline) 83ft 2in (25.35m); draught 25ft 11.5in (7.91m)
Machinery:	nine Babcock & Wilcox boilers, driving Parsons four-shaft turbines, developing 120,000hp
Maximum speed:	32.5kt
Armour:	belt 2.5in to 4in (63mm to 102mm); armour deck 1.5in (38mm); bulkheads 4in (102mm)
Armament:	eight 5in (127mm) guns, 16 28mm guns, 24 12.7mm machine gun launchers, plus 80 aircraft (standard)
Complement:	2175
Country:	USA

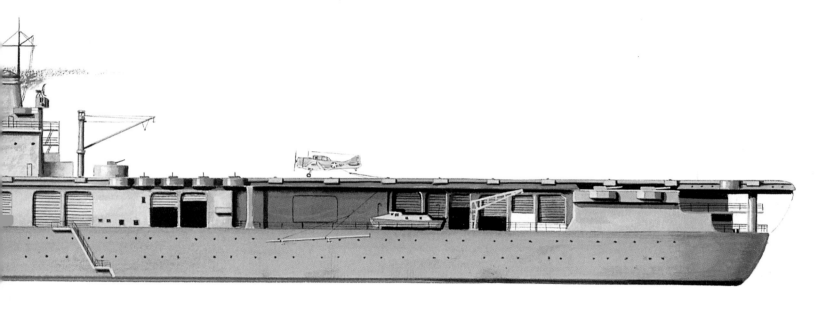

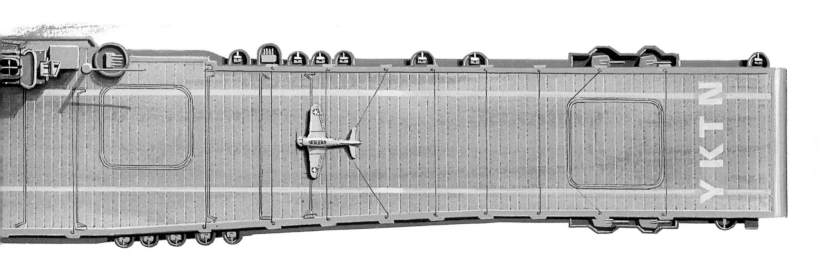

Zuiho

As part of a shadow shipbuilding programme to get around Washington Treaty restrictions, Japan built two submarine depot ships, named *Takasaki* and *Tsurugisaki*, which could be converted to fleet oilers or small aircraft carriers in time of war. In the event *Tsurugisaki* (the first to be laid down) was built as a depot ship, but *Takasagi* was modified to carrier status while still in the yard. At that point she was renamed *Zuiho*. Her sister-ship did not follow this route, becoming the carrier *Shoho*. Because of the disparity in the ships' histories the two carriers are referred to in various sources as both the *Zuiho* and *Shoho* class – *Zuiho* was built first, but *Shoho* was the first to become a carrier. *Zuiho* was laid down on 20 June 1935 (six months after *Shoho*), launched on 19 June 1936 and commissioned on 27 December 1940. As submarine tenders, the two vessels already had a seaplane

hangar, and this was simply extended for their new role. New machinery was fitted to give them more speed. Two lifts were added to the flight deck, no island was built and the smokestack curved down to one side, in the standard Japanese fashion. *Shoho* was an early Japanese loss, sunk during the Battle of the Coral Sea. *Zuiho* had a longer career, starting the war with the East Indies invasions of 1942. She was attacked and damaged by aircraft from USS *Enterprise* in October 1942, but returned to duty after repair. *Zuiho* went on to see action in the Guadalcanal and Marianas campaigns, during December 1942 and June 1943, but was finally sunk during the Leyte Gulf battles. On 25 October 1944 aircraft from the US Navy's Task Force 38 caught up with *Zuiho* at Cape Engaño, and scored a succession of torpedo and bomb hits to sink the Japanese carrier.

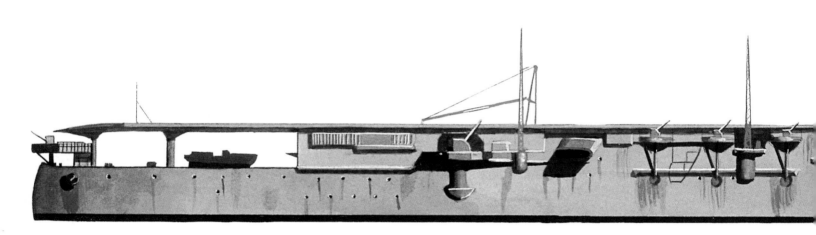

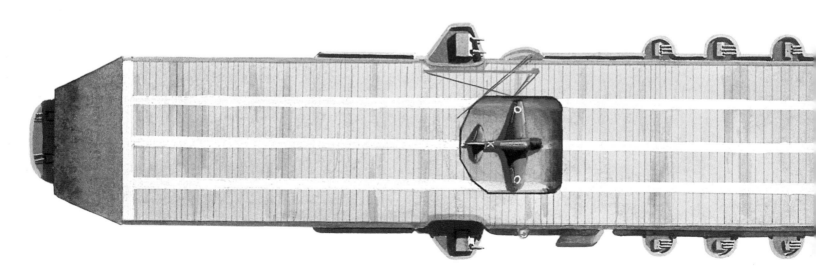

Aircraft carriers

Specification
Displacement: 11,262t standard; 13,730t full load
Dimensions: length (overall) 671ft 11in (204.8m); beam (at the waterline) 59ft 9in (18.21m); draught 21ft 9in (6.68m)
Machinery: four Kampon boilers, driving two-shaft geared turbines, developing 52,000hp
Maximum speed: 28kt
Armour: none
Armament: eight 5in (127mm) guns, eight 25mm guns, plus 30 aircraft (standard)
Complement: 785
Country: Japan

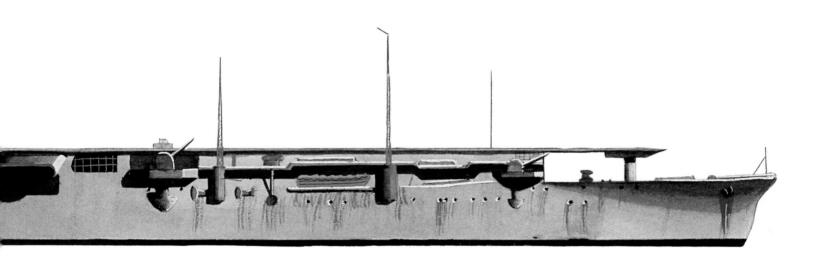

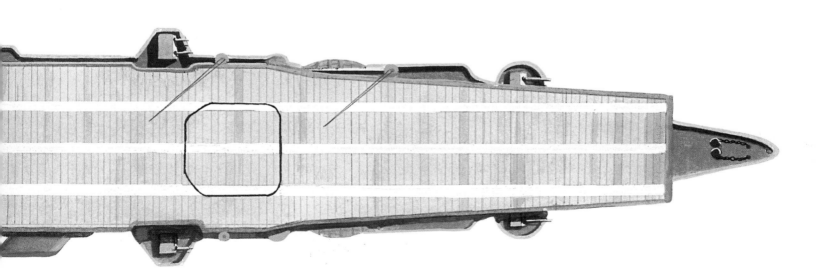

Admiral Graf Spee

The Treaty of Versailles that followed World War I in 1919 placed heavy restrictions on the German navy. Germany was prohibited from building large capital ships and from developing a blue-water fleet. Only ships of less than 10,000 tons, armed with 11in (280mm) guns, were permitted. With these restrictions in place, the Allied powers reckoned that the German navy would be confined to operations within the Baltic, and thus pose no real threat in the future. However, the German planners of the late 1920s had other ideas. As new maritime technologies like electric welding and diesel powerplants became available it was possible to build smaller, faster, and far more effective warships than was hitherto believed possible. Though they were lightly armoured, when tasked with commerce raiding they posed a major threat to shipping. To the Kriegsmarine these innovative ships were the *Panzerschiffe* – literally armoured ships – but to the rest of the world they would become known as the 'pocket battleships'. The first to appear were the *Deutschland*-class, more correctly viewed as heavy cruisers. The three vessels in the class were larger than the Treaty terms allowed, at about 12,000 tons, and they retained the modest 11in (280mm) guns. Five larger *Hipper*-class *Panzerschiffe* would follow, but the *Deutschlands*

were first. *Admiral Graf Spee* was the third to be built with the *Admiral Scheer* and *Deutschland* preceding it over a period of three years. *Admiral Graf Spee* was laid down on 1 October 1932, launched on 30 June 1934 and commissioned on 6 January 1939. With the outbreak of war all three ships were quickly in action; indeed the *Graf Spee* had been deployed to the South Atlantic on 21 August 1939. Within months of Germany's declaration of war *Graf Spee* had cut a swathe of destruction through the Atlantic convoys, sinking over 50,000 tons of shipping. The Royal Navy gave chase and the cruisers *Exeter*, *Achilles* and *Ajax* were committed to hunt down the raider. In one of the great feats of wartime seamanship, the three smaller British cruisers – which were easily outgunned and outrun by *Graf Spee* – managed to damage and corner the German cruiser in the Rio de la Plata estuary, at Montevideo, in Uruguay. There the German commander was convinced by British Intelligence that a far larger naval force was awaiting his return. As a result he scuttled his ship and *Graf Spee* was sent to the bottom on 17 December 1939. After this sinking Hitler ordered the *Deutschland* to be renamed as *Lützow,* to avoid any risk of a ship named after the Fatherland suffering the same fate.

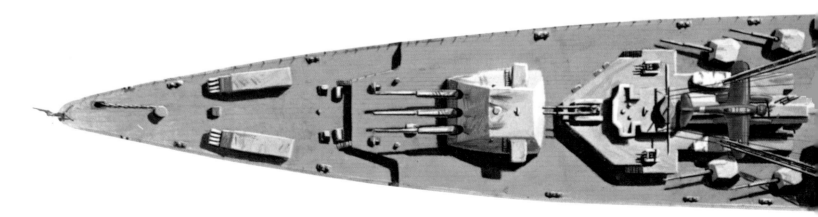

Battleships and Battlecruisers

Specification

Displacement:	11,700t standard; 16,200t deep load
Dimensions:	length (overall) 610ft 3in (186m); beam (at the waterline) 70ft 10in (21.59m); draught 24ft 3in (7.39m)
Machinery:	eight double-action two-stroke MAN nine-cylinder diesel engines, driving three-shafts, developing 54,000hp
Maximum speed:	28kt
Armour:	belt 3in to 2.25in (76mm to 57mm); deck 1.5in (38mm); torpedo bulkhead 1.75in to 1.5in (44mm to 38mm); main turrets 5.5in to 3.25in (140mm to 82mm)
Armament:	eight 11in (280mm) main guns, eight 6in (152mm) secondary guns, six 4.1in (105mm) guns, eight 37mm AA guns, six 20mm AA guns, eight 21in (533mm) torpedo tubes plus two aircraft
Complement:	619 to 1150
Country:	Germany

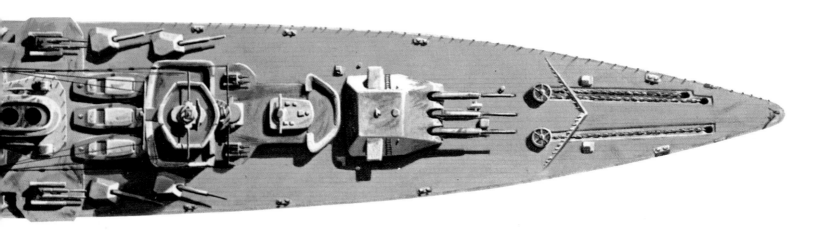

Bismarck

After Hitler's rise to power, renewed ship construction was begun in secret and, as Nazi Germany became more bellicose, a massive naval expansion plan was put into effect by the late 1930s. This 'Z-plan' called for the building of eight battleships, five battlecruisers, four aircraft carriers and 12 smaller cruisers. The lead ships in this programme would be the battleships *Bismarck* and *Tirpitz*. The Anglo-German Naval Agreement of 1935 permitted Germany to build two 35,000-ton battleships, but *Bismarck* and *Tirpitz* were secretly built much larger. Much of *Bismarck*'s basic design was based on Germany's *Baden*-class battleships of World War I, and some of the outdated features of those ships made their way into the new vessels. Several vital areas of the ship, such as its rudders, steering gear, radio and other communications systems, were left almost unprotected. Nor was the quality of *Bismarck*'s own shells very good, and many of those fired in anger failed to explode. However, *Bismarck* was intended to act as a surface raider and not to meet the Royal Navy in a straight fight. For this role she was an excellent ship. She was very well-built and generally well-armed with modern and efficient fire directors and six ship-borne Arado Ar 196 reconnaissance aircraft. Her 15in (381mm) main armament was adequate and equivalent to that of contemporary French and Italian battleships. *Bismarck* was laid down on 1 June 1936, launched on 14 February 1939 and commissioned on 24 August 1940. By May 1941 she was in the North Atlantic, with the cruiser *Prinz Eugen*, but her first foray into the war would prove to be her last. *Bismarck* had not sighted a single Allied convoy before the Royal Navy was on her trail. Pursued by the Home Fleet, *Bismarck* sank the battlecruiser HMS *Hood*, a tribute to the fire-direction skills of the German crew who, on paper, were outgunned. In one of the most devastating British losses of the war *Hood* blew up after a salvo from *Bismarck* – only three survived from a crew of over 1150. *Bismarck* attempted to escape back to France but was located and heroically attacked by torpedo-carrying Swordfish aircraft from HMS *Ark Royal*. These attacks damaged *Bismarck*'s rudder, exposing one of the vessel's basic design flaws, and *Bismarck* was found by the battleships HMS *King George V* and HMS *Rodney*, then finally sunk, on 27 May 1941, by torpedoes from the cruiser HMS *Dorsetshire*. *Bismarck*'s loss was to have a huge effect on the rest of the small German surface fleet, which was withdrawn to safer waters nearer home and never again became a factor in the wider war at sea.

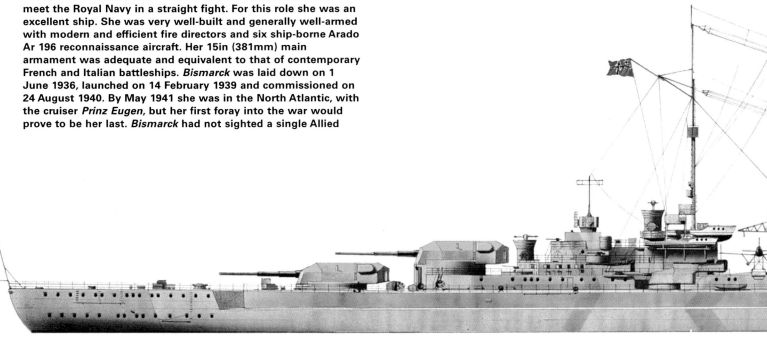

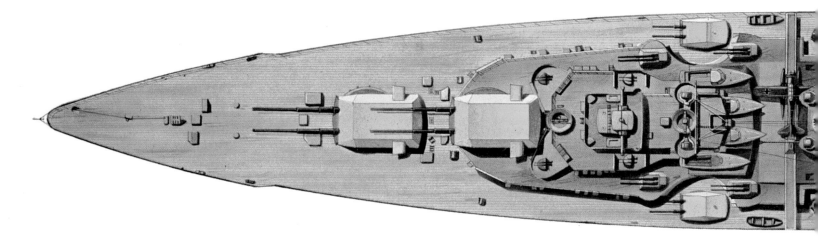

Specification

Displacement:	41,700t standard; 50,900t deep load
Dimensions:	length (overall) 813ft 8in (248m); beam (at the waterline) 118ft 1in (35.99m); draught 28ft 6in (8.68m)
Machinery:	12 Wagner boilers driving three-shaft Blohm & Voss turbines, developing 138,000hp
Maximum speed:	29kt
Armour:	belt 12.5in to 10.5in (317mm to 266mm); deck 2in (50mm); armoured deck 4.75in to 3.5in (119mm to 89mm); torpedo bulkhead 1.75in (44mm); slopes 4in (102mm); main turrets 14.5in to 7in (368mm to 178mm); secondary turrets 4in to 1.5in (102mm to 38mm)
Armament:	eight 15in (381mm) main guns, 12 6in (152mm) secondary guns, 16 4.1in (105mm) guns, 15 37mm AA guns, 12 20mm AA guns, plus four to six aircraft
Complement:	2092
Country:	Germany

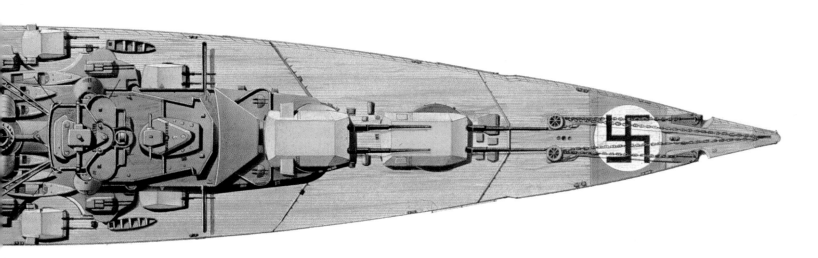

Dunkerque

Dunkerque was a product of the hasty French shipbuilding programme of the early 1930s, and introduced several new design concepts to the field. After a prolonged period of inaction between the wars, the French navy was driven by Germany's expansionist plans to improve its own naval forces. The *Dunkerque*-class ships were built in answer to Germany's own *Deutschland*-class cruisers. *Dunkerque* and her sister-ship *Strasbourg* were conceived as battleships but their fast, lightly-armoured configuration led to them being termed battlecruisers or 'fast battleships'. Their design set a trend that others would follow, particularly in Europe. The basic configuration of *Dunkerque* was inspired by the British *Nelson* class, with all the 13in (330mm) main guns mounted forward, in quadruple turrets, and a tower bridge structure. The advantage of positioning the main armament forward was that it allowed the magazines to be concentrated in one place and so saved weight. However, it restricted the ship's overall arc of fire and also left the turrets vulnerable to being put out of action by a single hit. The turrets were well-spaced to minimise this risk. *Dunkerque* was not heavily armoured, and was designed to resist an 11in (280mm)

shell fired from 18,000yds (16,640m). Protection from torpedoes was of more importance and the battlecruiser was fitted with a layer of underwater compartments filled with fuel, air and a rubber compound. Provision was made for two Loiré 130 floatplanes. *Dunkerque* was laid down on 24 December 1932, launched on 2 October 1935 and commissioned in April 1937. Before the French surrender both *Dunkerque* and *Strasbourg* undertook convoy protection duties. After France's capitulation to the Nazis, both ships were among the many French vessels in port outside Vichy French control. A decision was taken by the British not to let the French fleet fall into German hands and, as a result, *Dunkerque* was heavily damaged by Royal Navy gunfire at Mers-el-Kebir (Oran) in April 1940. On 6 July she was attacked again by Swordfish from HMS *Ark Royal,* and was very badly damaged when a barge carrying fuel and depth charges exploded beside her. *Dunkerque* eventually managed to limp back to port at Toulon in February 1942. There she was finally scuttled in dry dock in November 1942. The wreck remained in place until it was removed in 1945. The remains of the ship were scrapped in 1958.

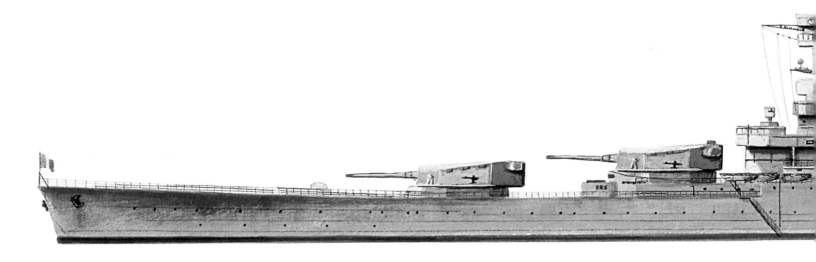

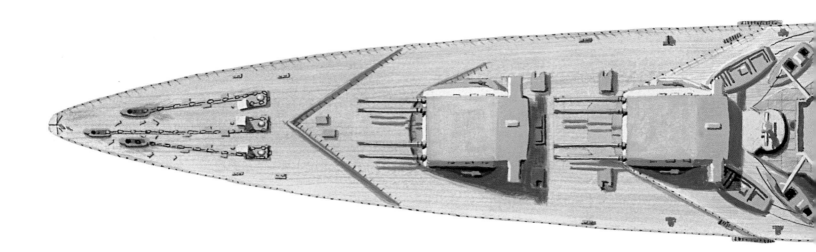

Battleships and Battlecruisers

Specification

Displacement:	26,500t standard; 30,750t deep load
Dimensions:	length (overall) 703ft 9in (214.5m); beam (at the waterline) 102ft (31m); draught 28ft 6in (8.68m)
Machinery:	six Indret boilers driving four-shaft Parson geared turbines, developing 112,500hp
Maximum speed:	29.5kt
Armour:	belt 9.75in to 5.75in (247mm to146mm); deck 5in to 1.5in (127mm to 38mm); torpedo bulkhead 1.5in (38mm); main turrets 13.25in to 6in (336mm to 152mm); secondary turrets 3.5in (89mm)
Armament:	eight 13in (330mm) main guns, 16 5.1in (130mm) secondary guns, eight 37mm AA guns, 32 13.2mm AA machine guns, plus two aircraft
Complement	1431
Country:	France

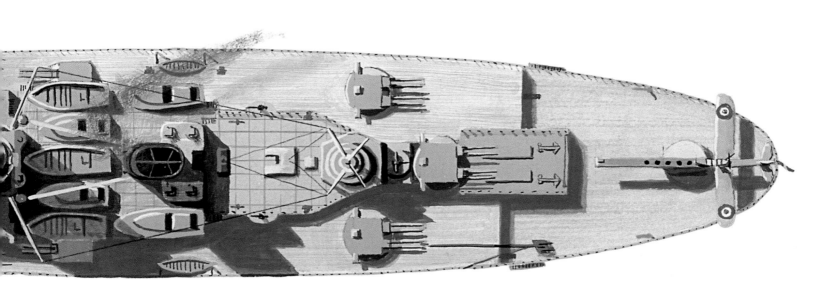

Gneisenau

Despite, or perhaps because of, their small numbers, the Kriegsmarine's big fighting ships were mythologised – by both sides – during World War II. The hunt for the *Bismarck* passed into popular folklore and the chase and sinking of the *Scharnhorst* and *Graf Spee* became other epic tales. *Scharnhorst*'s less famous sister-ship was *Gneisenau,* though both vessels were noteworthy. The design of the two ships was driven by Hitler himself who felt that the armament and speed of his 'pocket battleships' – the *Deutschland-* and *Hipper*-class cruisers – could be incorporated into larger, better-armoured vessels, thus creating the perfect blend of offensive and defensive capabilities. With their extra armour, Hitler saw these ships as 'unsinkable commerce raiders', but to the navy they were simply larger, and definitely underarmed, warships. The navy insisted that a third triple main turret be added to the design at the very least. Hitler was reluctant to do this for fear of antagonising the British – he had wanted the ships to appear

innocuous – but the design change was finally forced through. It was initially planned to equip these *Panzerschiffe* (armoured ships) with 15in (381mm) guns (though under the Anglo-German Naval Treaty of 1935 they could have carried a 16in (406mm) main armament without censure). However, the new 15in (381mm) triple turret design was not yet ready and so the two *Scharnhorst*-class battlecruisers were built with 11in (280mm) guns to save time. *Gneisenau* was laid down on 3 May 1935, launched on 8 December 1936 and commissioned on 21 May 1938. *Scharnhorst* was laid down a few days later, launched six months sooner but was only commissioned in January 1939. In the winter of 1938–39 each ship was refitted with a rakish clipper bow, seaplane catapults were added and additional 20mm AA guns appeared. After the outbreak of war *Gneisenau* still had its inadequate 11in (280mm) guns in place. *Gneisenau* covered the German landings in Norway and saw action in the Atlantic. Aided by *Scharnhorst*, she was

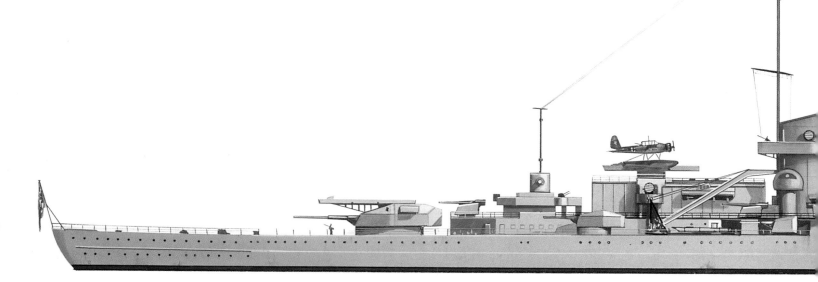

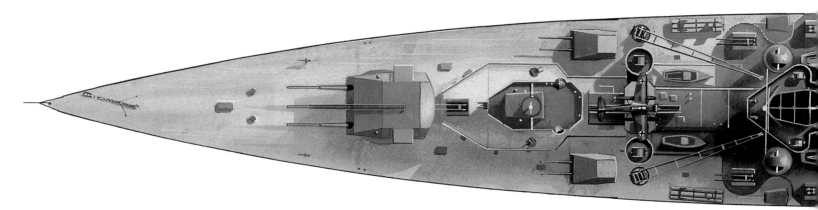

responsible for the sinking of the British carrier HMS *Glorious* along with the destroyers HMS *Acasta* and HMS *Ardent*. On 6 April 1941, *Gneisenau* was struck by a torpedo and having been towed back to harbour, was hit again by four bombs in a British raid. When the ship was damaged a second time by an RAF air raid on Kiel in November 1942, the decision was taken to fit the proper 15in (381mm) guns, but these never arrived. Plans to refit the new turrets were abandoned in 1943, and *Gneisenau*'s main armament ended up as coastal batteries in Holland and Norway. Even the 6in (152mm) secondary guns were taken away and used, in one case, as railway guns. *Gneisenau* played no further part in the war. While *Scharnhorst* was sunk in December 1943 in an intense battle with three British cruisers and a battleship, *Gneisenau* was towed into the (now) Polish port of Gotenhafen (Gdynia) and scuttled to block the harbour entrance in 1945. After the war the wreck was broken up between 1947 and 1951.

Specification

Displacement:	34,841t standard; 38,900t deep load
Dimensions:	length (overall) 753ft 11in (229.79m); beam (at the waterline) 98ft 5in (29.92m); draught 27ft 6in (8.38m)
Machinery:	12 Wagner boilers driving three-shaft Germania geared turbines, developing 165,000hp
Maximum speed:	32kt
Armour:	belt 13.75in to 6.75in (349mm to 169mm); deck 2in (50mm); armoured deck 3in (76mm); torpedo bulkhead 1.75in (44mm); main turrets 14in to 6in (356mm to 152mm); secondary turrets 5.5in to 2in (140mm to 50mm)
Armament:	nine 11in (280mm) main guns, 12 6in (152mm) secondary guns, 14 4.1in (105mm) guns, 16 37mm AA guns, eight 20mm AA guns, plus three to four aircraft
Complement:	1669
Country:	Germany

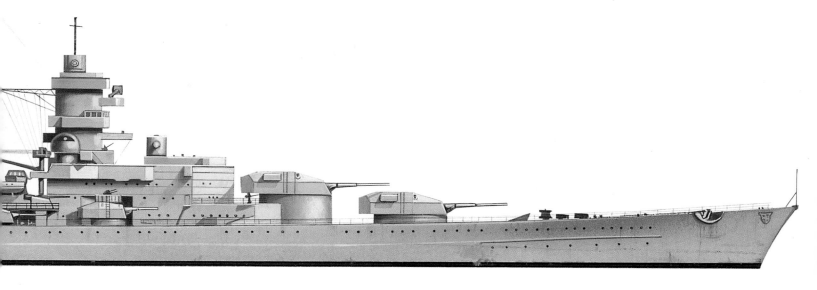

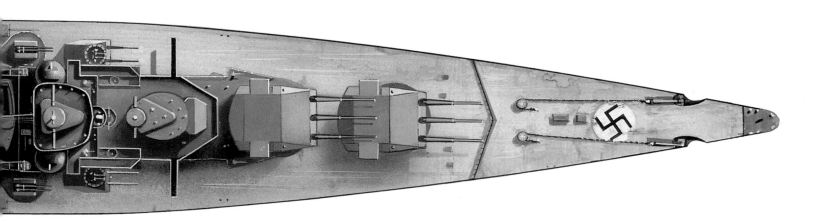

HMS *Hood*

When she was launched, HMS *Hood* was a ship apart, and throughout her life glamour and publicity accompanied the vessel. For its day, *Hood* was a masterful ship with many fine features, but the design was rooted in World War I, and this was the reason for her spectacular loss some 25 years or so later. Spurred by German advances, in 1915 the British Admiralty drew up plans for a new class of fast, well-armed and well-armoured battlecruisers. The designs that emerged were better armed than the *Queen Elizabeth*-class battleships, and faster too, but armour protection had taken a low priority. Orders were placed for four ships but in the aftermath of the Battle of Jutland in May 1916 it was starkly evident that these *Hood*-class battlecruisers would be extremely vulnerable in any future naval battle. The battlecruiser approach was abandoned, and the ships were

redesigned as 'fast battleships' with much more armour. With the end of the war in 1918, all but HMS *Hood* were cancelled, and the ship was hailed as a great step forward. In fact, *Hood* was a mix of old and new features. For example, she boasted modern inclined armour and good anti-torpedo protection, high-angle long-range main guns and powerful small-tube boilers. On the other hand, she also had the dubious distinction of being the last British capital ship with open secondary turrets, which were poorly positioned – none of the original 5.5in (140mm) guns fitted could be trained on the beam. She was also top-heavy and slow. HMS *Hood* was laid down on 1 September 1916, launched on 22 August 1918 and commissioned in 1920. In the following years, *Hood* underwent little in the way of modernisation, with the only changes affecting her AA armament. By late 1939, new

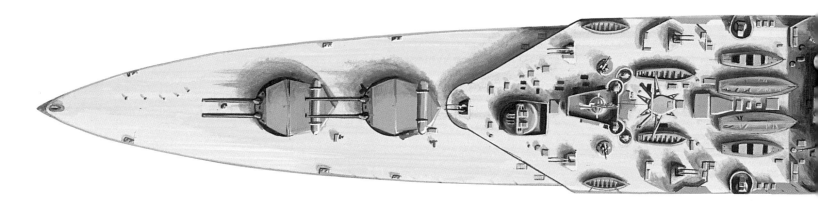

4in (102mm) AA guns were added and the unsatisfactory 5.5in (140mm) guns were removed and replaced with six 4in (102mm) guns, in different mounts. Having seen little action in the early stages of the war, *Hood* was one of the leading vessels devoted to the hunt for the *Bismarck*. The inferiority of her 1916-vintage design became all too apparent when she engaged *Bismarck* on 23 May 1941, and was destroyed by a handful of shells – perhaps only one – from the German battleship. A salvo from *Bismarck* landed between *Hood*'s second funnel and the main mast. A direct hit was scored on one of her magazines (or perhaps a boiler) and *Hood* disappeared in a huge explosion that left only three of her crew of nearly 1500 alive.

Specification

Displacement:	41,200t standard; 44,600t deep load
Dimensions:	length (overall) 860ft 7in (262.3m); beam (at the waterline) 105ft 2.5in (32.06m); draught 31ft 6in (9.6m)
Machinery:	24 Yarrow boilers driving four four-shaft Brown and Curtis geared turbines, developing 151,280hp
Maximum speed:	29.5kt
Armour:	belt 9.75in to 5.75in (247mm to 146mm); deck 5in to 1.5in (127mm to 38mm); torpedo bulkhead 1.5in (38mm); main turrets 13.25in to 6in (336mm to 152mm); secondary turrets 3.5in (89mm)
Armament:	eight 13in (330mm) main guns, 16 5.1in (130mm) secondary guns, eight 37mm AA guns, 32 13.2mm AA machine guns, plus two aircraft
Complement:	1477
Country:	GB

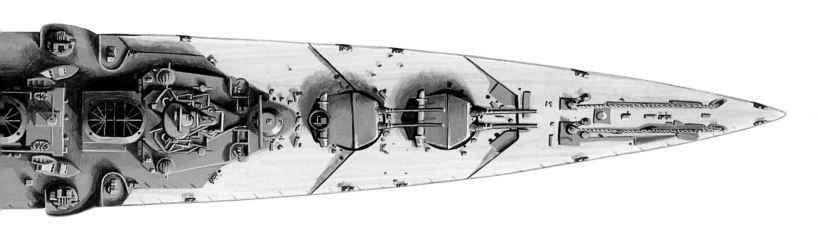

HMS *Howe*

When faced with the decision to build the *King George V*-class battleships, the Royal Navy found itself in a quandary. In the early-1930s Britain was still bound by the Washington Treaty limitations of 1922, which forbade the development of capital ships larger than 35,000 tons or with guns above 16in (406mm) calibre. By 1934 Britain had plans for ships with nine 15in (381mm) guns but it seemed certain that Japan would no longer abide by the Treaty, and Germany was also drawing up plans for its *Bismarck*-class ships. While Britain did not want to be left behind, neither did it want to provide an excuse for the other navies to step outside the prescribed limits. The Royal Navy had to make a decision with this in mind, while all the time knowing that it could be at war with Germany by the time the new ships were ready for service. The final *King George V* design was ready by 1936. Britain opted for 14in (356mm) guns but with armour capable of resisting 16in (406mm) shells. It had originally been intended to fit 12 main guns, but to increase the level of armour protection two guns were deleted on the forward 'B' turret. Much effort was spent on designing and developing the ships' armour and the five battleships of the class had extensive

armour belts and internal bulkheads. Submarine protection proved to be less satisfactory, however. The only member of the class to be lost during World War II – HMS *Prince of Wales* – was sunk by a small and outdated German torpedo. HMS *Howe* (formerly HMS *Beatty*) was laid down on 1 June 1937, launched on 9 April 1940 and completed on 29 August 1942. The other *King George V*s were involved in several major actions including the *Bismarck* and *Scharnhorst* engagements, but *Howe* fought a solid war away from the front pages. Along with HMS *King George V*, HMS *Duke of York* and HMS *Anson*, *Howe* outlasted the war and remained in front-line service alongside her sisters into the 1950s. All four vessels were finally broken up between 1957 and 1958.

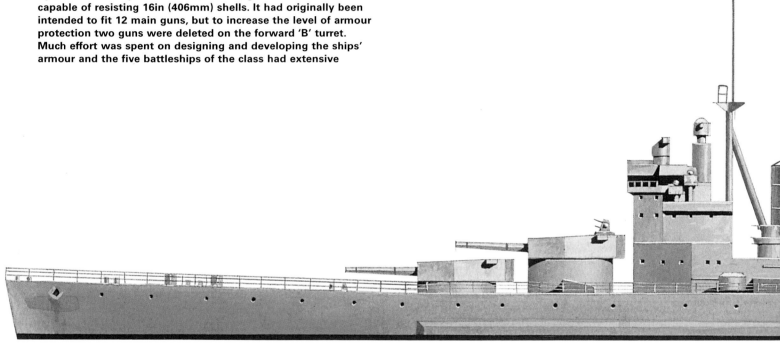

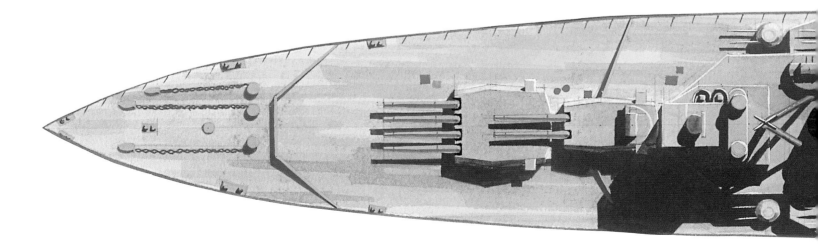

Battleships and Battlecruisers

Specification

Displacement:	36,727t standard; 42,076t deep load
Dimensions:	length (overall) 745ft (227m); beam (at the waterline) 103ft (31.4m); draught 32ft 7in (9.93m)
Machinery:	eight Admiralty three-drum boilers, driving four-shaft Parsons geared turbines, developing 110,000 hp
Maximum speed:	29.5kt
Armour:	belt 15in to 4.5in (381mm to 115mm); bulkheads 12in to 4in (305mm to 102mm); main turrets 13in to 6in (330mm to 152mm)
Armament:	10 14in (406mm) main guns, 16 5.25in (133mm) secondary guns, 32 two-pounder 'pom pom' AA guns, 14 40mm Bofors AA guns, 65 20mm Oerlikon AA guns, plus two aircraft (removed 1943–45)
Complement:	1422
Country:	GB

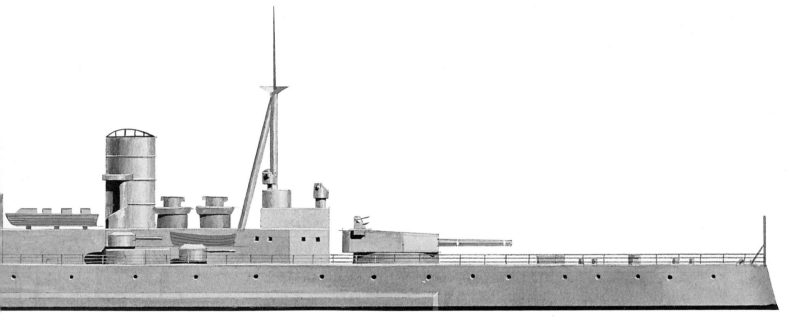

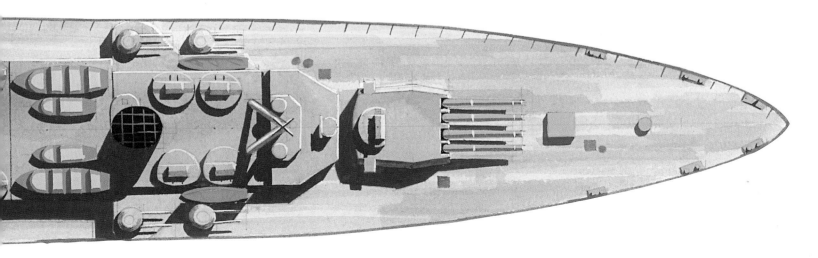

USS *Iowa* (BB-61)

The four *Iowa*-class battleships were the largest and fastest to serve with the US Navy during World War II and they remain among the most imposing and effective combat vessels afloat. In 1936, freed from many of the restrictions of the 1922 Washington Treaty, the US Navy embarked on a programme to build a new class of 45,000-ton ships. They were a step forward from the preceding *South Dakota* class and incorporated many modern design improvements. While they retained the same basic armament the new ships were much better armoured and faster. In fact, with a maximum speed of some 33kt, the *Iowas* were the fastest battleships ever built. A new type of 16in (406mm) gun was fitted – a 50 calibre gun as opposed to the 45-calibre guns used previously. The *Iowas* also featured a new main turret design that saved about 850 tons in weight. The driving principle behind the class design was the US concept of fast task forces operating in the Pacific. US planners correctly assumed that in any future war Japan would form similar groups and use them to attack supply ships crossing the Pacific. The *Iowa*-class battleships were intended to operate with US carriers and protect them while they attacked the Japanese surface units. A total of six was planned but only four were built: the USS *Iowa*, USS *New Jersey*, USS *Missouri* and the USS *Wisconsin*. The *Iowa* was laid down on 27 June 1940, launched

on 27 August 1942 and commissioned on 22 February 1943. They did not enter service until the latter half of the war and so missed many of the large carrier-versus-carrier engagements where they could have fulfilled their intended role. Nevertheless, the *Iowa*-class ships operated with great distinction as part of the US Navy Fast Carrier Task Force, often as command ships. Each battleship differed in detail, particularly in specific AA armament which changed continuously throughout the war. All had a successful war in the Pacific – the Japanese surrender was signed aboard the USS *Missouri* – and none were lost. In 1943 the USS *Iowa* was involved in the 'Tirpitz watch' and in November she carried President Roosevelt to the Teheran conference. On 23 January 1944 *Iowa*'s war began in earnest when she participated in the strikes on the Marshall Islands. Off Truk Island she sank the Japanese cruiser *Katori,* and then continued to support operations throughout the Philippines until the Battle of Leyte Gulf in October. On her way home to port in December 1944, *Iowa* survived a typhoon that sunk or damaged 24 other ships. Returning to combat in April 1945, she relieved the USS *New Jersey* off Okinawa. By July 1945 the three available *Iowa*-class ships were shelling targets on the Japanese mainland and, on 29 August 1945, *Iowa* sailed into Tokyo harbour with the *Missouri* to accept the Japanese surrender. The *Iowa*s

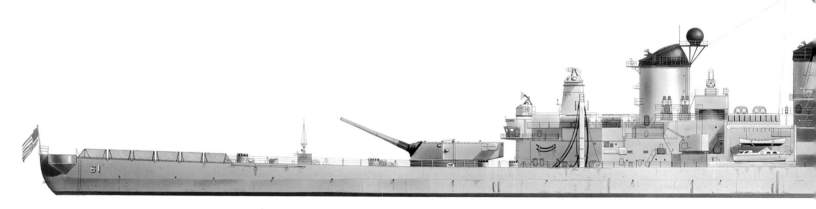

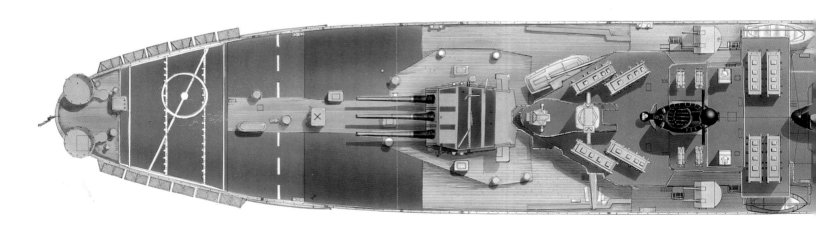

were popular with their crews and proved very manoeuvrable vessels, despite their great length. They were, however, expensive to operate and were mothballed soon after the war. Held in the US Navy's Reserve fleet, the combat power of the *Iowa*s could not be ignored. They were reactivated for fire support duties in the Korean war and then again during the Vietnam war. Mothballed a third time in the early 1970s, they were recommissioned in the free-spending Reagan years to become symbols of America's military power and prestige. At one time it was planned to convert them to hybrid VSTOL aircraft carriers, with a flight deck on the rear fuselage. This was never carried out but they were rearmed with Tomahawk cruise missiles and Harpoon anti-ship missiles, while still retaining their highly accurate 16in (406mm) main guns (as shown below). The *Iowa* made a show of force off Nicaragua in 1984 and served as a tanker escort in the Persian Gulf in 1988. The other battleships undertook fire support duties off the Lebanon during the 1980s and then action against Iraqi targets in Kuwait during Operation Desert Storm. In 1989, *Iowa* suffered an explosion in one of her main turrets which kept her out of Desert Storm and led to her decommissioning in October 1990. The four *Iowa*-class ships are now held in reserve awaiting a decision on their fate.

Specification

Displacement:	48,110t standard; 57,540t deep load
Dimensions:	length (overall) 887ft 3in (270.43m); beam (at the waterline) 108ft 2in (32.97m); draught 36ft 2.25in (11.02m)
Machinery:	eight Babcock & Wilcox boilers driving four-shaft General Electric turbines, developing 212,000hp
Maximum speed:	33kt
Armour:	belt 12in to 1.6in (305mm to 40mm); armoured deck 6in to 1.5in (152mm to 38mm); bulkheads 11.3in (287mm); main turrets 19.7in (500mm)
Armament:	nine 16in (406mm) main guns, 20 5in (127mm) secondary guns, 60 40mm AA guns, 60 20mm AA guns, plus three aircraft
Complement:	1921
Country:	USA

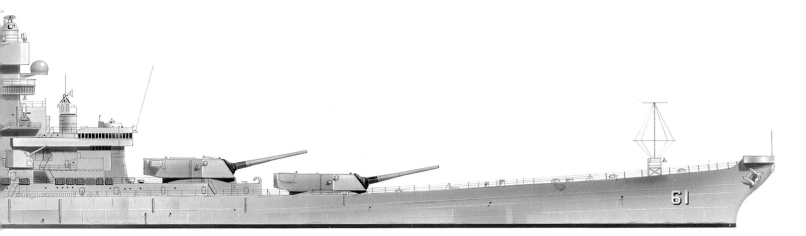

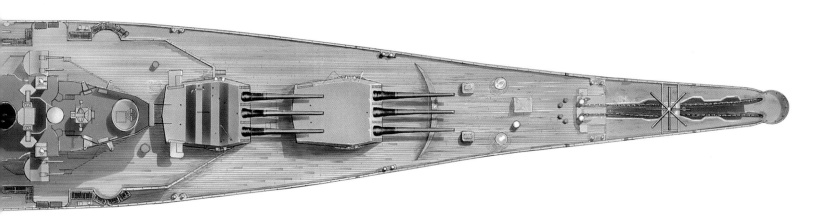

Ise

When it was launched in 1914, *Fuso* – and her sistership of 1915, *Yamashiro* – were the most powerful battleships in the Japanese Navy. In 1916 and 1917 they were joined by two more vessels in the same class, *Ise* and *Hyuga*. They outgunned most of their US Navy rivals and matched the *Pennsylvania*-class battleships. The arrival of these ships marked Japan's coming of age as a major naval power. *Fuso*'s 14in (356mm) main guns were made in Japan, another first for the navy, and the gun turrets were arranged in an unusual fashion – two fore and two aft, but two amidships also. By the time war came to the Pacific the *Ise* and her sisterships had been remodelled and upgraded several times. Between 1935 and 1937 the ship was fitted with built-up foremasts and 3.1in (77mm) AA guns. *Fuso* underwent a fairly extensive rebuild between 1930 and 1935, with substantial 'pagoda'-style masts replacing the forward funnel, the main mast was further built up and large amounts of extra armour were added, on the deck and underwater. As a result the weight of the ship increased by about 3500t and the hull was extended aft. Completely new machinery was fitted with more powerful Kampon turbines replacing the original Brown-Curtis powerplants. Additional light armament was progressively fitted and the *Fuso* could also carry up to three seaplanes (typically Nakajima Type 95s). Japan's capital ships did not play a great part in the Pacific campaign after their support for the initial invasions that swept across the region. Following the losses at Midway, in 1943 the *Ise* and *Hyuga* were converted into hybrid battleship-aircraft carriers. The rear X and Y turrets were removed and the aircraft launched by catapult and recovered from the sea by

crane. These ships were capable of carrying 22 seaplanes, but they were not a success. More and more anti-aircraft armament was added until *Ise* had over 100 25mm AA guns, compared to the 16 with which she was built. At the same time the secondary main armament was all removed. *Ise*'s air group had neither the range nor the firepower needed to be a significant asset, and by the end of the war its catapults had been removed, and the ship operated without aircraft at Leyte Gulf. *Ise* was sunk, near Kure, by US carrier warplanes on 18 July 1945. The *Hyuga* was lost just six days later. Both ships sank in shallow water and were broken up after 1945.

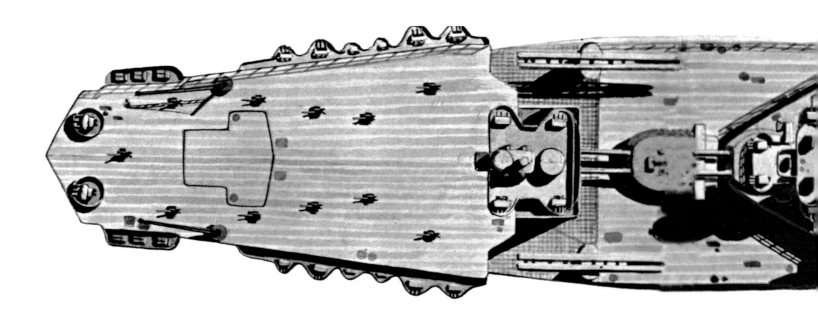

Battleships and Battlecruisers

Specification

Displacement:	35,350t standard; 38,065t trial
Dimensions:	length (overall) 720ft 5in (219.5m); beam (at the waterline) 100ft 6in (30.6m); draught 29ft 7in (9m)
Machinery:	eight Kampon boilers, driving four-shaft Kampon geared turbines, developing 80,000hp
Maximum speed:	25.3kt
Armour:	belt 12in to 4in (305mm to 102mm)
Armament:	eight 14in (356mm) main guns, 16 5in (127mm) guns, two 3.1in (77mm) AA guns, 104 25mm AA guns plus 22 aircraft
Complement:	1463
Country:	Japan

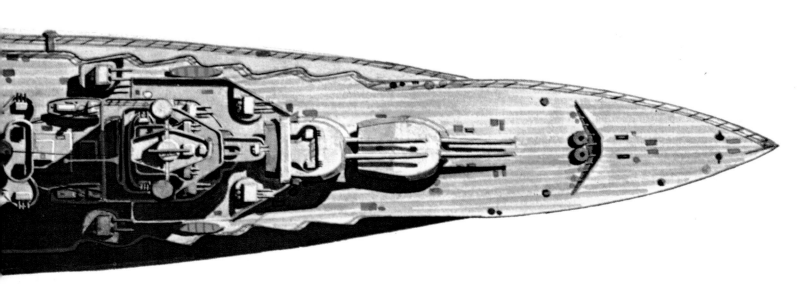

Littorio

The arms accords that had governed capital ship development among the major maritime powers began to break down during the 1930s. Some nations began to test the limits of treaties, while others broke them outright. When France began work on new battlecruisers, Fascist Italy felt compelled to begin its own naval renaissance, laying down the *Littorio*-class battleships. These vessels were the first true battleships to be built in Europe since 1922, and the first capital ships to be built in Italy since the end of World War I. The *Littorio* class consisted of two batches each of two ships, laid down in 1934 and 1938 respectively. *Littorio* and her sister-ship *Vittorio Veneto* were laid down on the same day and the names of both ships have been used interchangeably to identify the class. In outline *Littorio* was a 35,000-ton vessel, but by the time of its launch it had grown

considerably. *Littorio* was armed with high-velocity 15in (381mm) guns, which was the largest calibre that could be reliably built in Italy at the time. Flanking the three main turrets were the secondary 6in (152mm) guns, mounted in four triple turrets. Separate 3.5in (89mm) AA guns were carried in single mounts along the ship's flanks along with additional 4.7in (119mm) guns. The rear main turret was mounted higher than normal to allow blast clearance for the ship's aircraft, typically a Regianne Re 2000 fighter, which was carried unhangared. In contrast to the panoply of armament, *Littorio* was no more than adequately armoured: speed was of more importance to her designers. However, torpedo protection was well thought-out and effective. *Littorio* was laid down on 28 October 1934, launched on 22 August 1937 (a month after *Vittorio Veneto*) and completed on

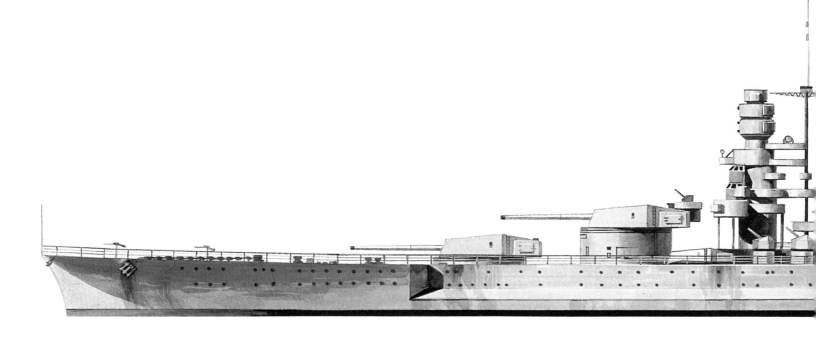

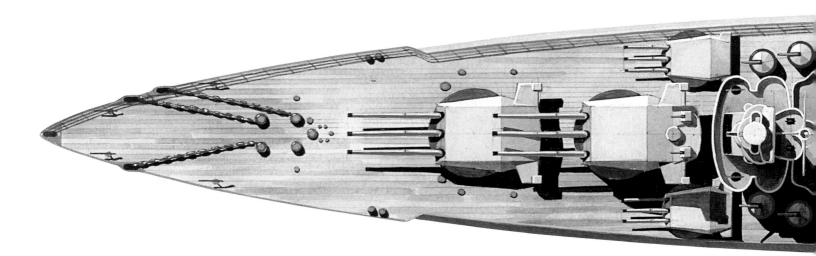

6 May 1940. *Littorio* was almost immediately in action and became embroiled in the Royal Navy's rout of the Italian fleet at Taranto. There, *Littorio* was hit by three torpedoes dropped by Fleet Air Arm Swordfish on 11 November 1940, but survived. Repairs lasted until April 1941, and after returning to action *Littorio* survived further damage at the Battle of Sirte in March 1942 and air attacks in June 1942 and April 1943. On 30 July 1943, five days after Mussolini's overthrow, *Littorio* was renamed *Italia*. While steaming to surrender in Malta, alongside *Roma* of the same class, she was hit by a German glider bomb on 9 September. *Roma* was sunk and *Italia* badly damaged. Put out of action, *Italia* survived the rest of the war, returning to Italy in 1946. She was assigned to the USA as war reparations and scrapped between 1948 and 1950.

Specification

Displacement:	40,724t standard; 45,236t deep load
Dimensions:	length (overall) 780ft (237.74m); beam (at the waterline) 105ft 7in (32.18m); draught 31ft 5in (9.57m)
Machinery:	eight Yarrow boilers, driving four-shaft Belluzzo turbines, developing 128,200hp
Maximum speed:	30kt
Armour:	belt 11in to 2.65in (280mm to 70mm); deck 6.37in to 1.75ins (162mm to 45mm); bulkheads 8.26in to 2.75in (210mm to 70mm); main turrets 13.78in to 7.87in (350mm to 200mm); secondary turrets 11in to 2.65in (280mm to 70mm)
Armament:	nine 15in (381mm) main guns, 12 6in (152mm) secondary guns, four 4.7in (119mm) guns, 12 3.5in (89mm) AA guns, 20 37mm AA guns, 16 20mm AA guns, plus aircraft
Complement:	1830 to 1950
Country:	Italy

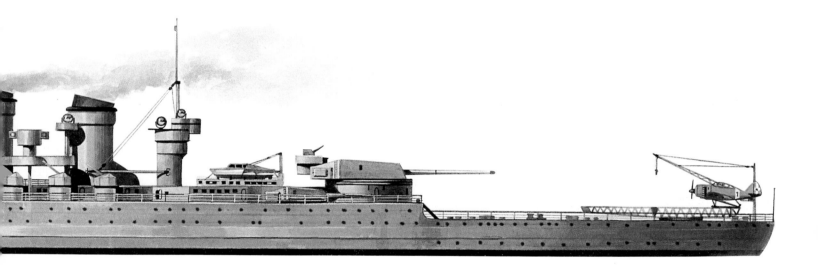

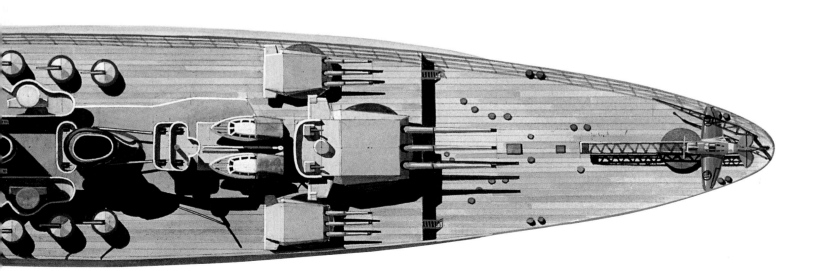

USS *Mississippi* (BB-41)

The three *New Mexico*-class battleships were based on the earlier *Pennsylvania* class and, as such, had their roots in pre-World War I battleship design. They were launched in 1917 but, despite their age at the advent of World War II, they proved to be durable and effective ships. The class introduced the first clipper bows to battleships in the US Navy. For the first time also the main guns were individually sleeved, allowing them to be independently raised. The USS *New Mexico* was built around a revolutionary turbo-electric drive, with steam turbines powering electric motors. Despite its bulk, and the obvious risks of having electric motors at sea, the system proved reliable and gave the ship good manoeuvrability. However, the other ships used conventional powerplants and *New Mexico* was refitted in the same way between 1931 and 1933. The USS *Mississippi* was the middle ship of the class, being followed by USS *Idaho*. She was

launched on 25 January 1917. By the 1930s new designs were appearing, but the only substantial improvements required by *Mississippi* and her sister vessels were changes to their underwater protection and the maximum elevation of the main guns, which was increased to 30°. *Mississippi* survived the attack on Pearl Harbor, after which her captain demanded a substantial increase in the ship's AA protection. The three *New Mexico*s saw extensive service with the US Navy during the war. By 1945 all of *Mississippi*'s old-fashioned design features, such as the two tall cage masts, had disappeared, while the funnels, bridge and superstructure had changed almost out of all recognition. All the non-AA 5in (127mm) guns were also removed. After the war *Mississippi* became a test and trials ship, and in 1952 she was fitted with the Terrier SAM system. The USS *Mississippi* was finally broken up in 1956.

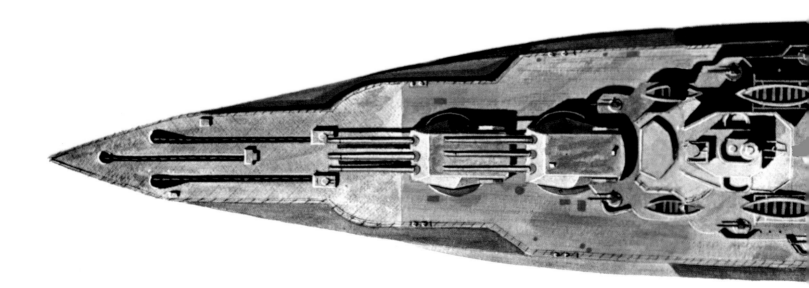

Battleships and Battlecruisers

Specification

Displacement: 32,000t standard; 33,500t deep load
Dimensions: length (overall) 624ft (190.2m); beam (at the waterline) 97ft 5in (26.7m); draught 34 ft (10.36m)
Machinery: nine Babcock boilers, driving Westinghouse geared turbines, developing 40,000hp
Maximum speed: 21kt
Armour: belt 14in to 8in (356mm to 203mm); deck 6in to 3in (152mm to 76mm); main turrets 18in to 9in (457mm to 229mm); secondary turrets 6in to 3in (152mm to 76mm)
Armament: 12 14in (356mm) main guns, 16 5in (127mm) secondary guns, 13 quadruple 40mm AA guns, 20 twin 20mm AA guns, plus two aircraft
Complement: 1084
Country: USA

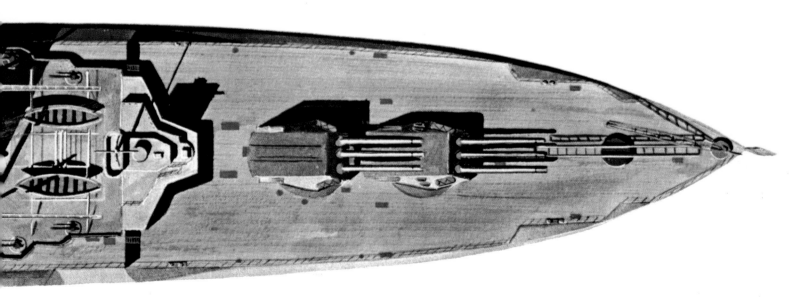

Nagato

Japan's *Nagato* class of 1917 opened a new era in battleship design. They introduced 16in (409mm) guns and possessed an excellent combination of speed and armour protection. With just eight of the larger guns, *Nagato* could fire a broadside with almost the same weight of shot as a battleship with 12 14in (356mm) guns (such as Japan's earlier *Hyuga*-class). Having fewer guns brought an important weight saving and *Nagato* still boasted 10 5.5in (130mm) guns as its secondary armament. *Nagato* also introduced the first of the distinctive 'pagoda' foremasts, on top of which was situated the fire control station. The only area in which *Nagato* was obviously lacking came in its machinery which, as it used mixed coal and oil firing, was not state-of-the-art. *Nagato* was launched on 19 November 1919, and was joined by a single sister-ship, *Mutsu*. Over the intervening years before the advent of war *Nagato* went through several modifications and changes. In 1924 the forefunnel was given a distinctive S-curve to stop smoke from obscuring the view from the control station. Major changes came between 1934 and 1936 when the stern was extended by 30ft (9.14m), a triple bottom and side bulges were added, 10 new oil-fired boilers were fitted, the S-curved funnel was removed (only one now remained) and new armament appeared. Several of the smaller guns were removed and those that remained had their elevation increased. A series of new AA guns were fitted and *Nagato* was fitted with a stern catapult for her own aircraft. The catapult and the shipboard aircraft were specifically developed by Germany's Ernst Heinkel. All this, plus new armour, saw tonnage increase by 6500 tons. *Nagato* and *Mutsu* saw considerable service throughout the war, though the latter was destroyed by an (accidental) internal explosion in June 1943. By 1945 *Nagato* was being used as a fixed AA ship armed with 98 25mm cannon and fitted with radar. By the end of the war the ship had sustained heavy damage and it was destroyed in the Crossroads atomic tests at Bikini Atoll, in 1946.

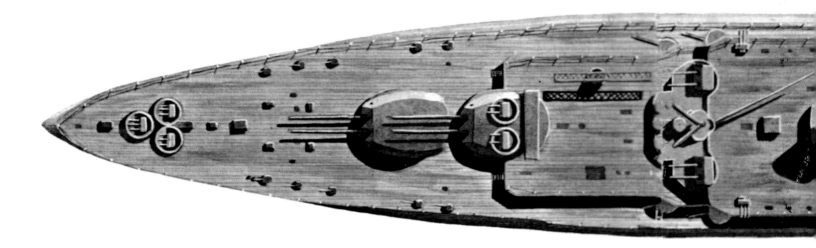

Battleships and Battlecruisers

Specification

Displacement:	39,120t standard; 42,753t deep load
Dimensions:	length (overall) 738ft (224.9m); beam (at the waterline) 108ft 2in (32.96m); draught 31ft 2in (9.5m)
Machinery:	10 boilers, driving four-shaft geared turbines, developing 82,000hp
Maximum speed:	25kt
Armour:	belt 11.8in (300mm); deck 5in to 2.7in (127mm to 68mm); main turrets 14in (356mm)
Armament:	eight 16.1in (409mm) main guns, eight 5.5in (140mm) secondary guns, eight 5in (127mm) dual-purpose guns, 68 25mm AA guns, plus three aircraft
Complement:	1368
Country:	Japan

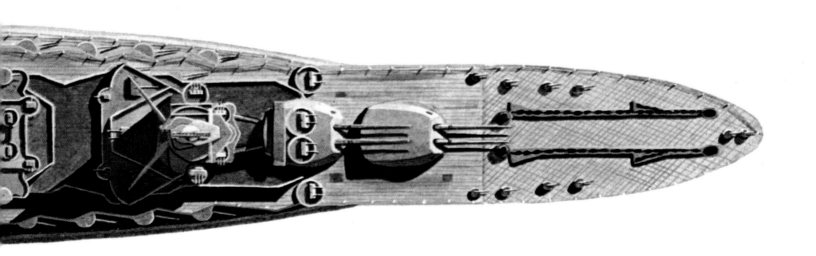

Richelieu

The *Richelieu*-class battleships were the finest ships built for the French navy before World War II. As German developments proceeded in the late 1920s and early 1930s, France feared that its new *Dunkerque*-class fast battleships (battlecruisers) would not be enough to maintain parity with the German fleet, so the French embarked on a fully-fledged battleship design of their own. The ensuing *Richelieu* class was based on the *Dunkerque* class, but fitted with 15in (381mm) guns and more heavily armoured. The original plan called for four *Richelieu*s, but events in the war meant that only three were ever laid down and only two were finished. *Richelieu*'s main guns were all fitted forward, in two quadruple turrets, while all the secondary guns, in five triple 6in (152mm) turrets, were mounted aft and amidships. In the main turrets the 15in (381mm) guns were mounted in pairs, capable of independent movement. The original designs for *Richelieu* featured a separate smokestack and control tower, but in the finished ship the two were fused together, with the funnel angled back to keep smoke away from the fire control station.

Richelieu was laid down on 22 October 1935 and launched on 17 January 1939. In June 1940, the ship was only 95 per cent finished when she steamed out of the shipyards at Arsénal de Brest to escape the German invasion. At the same time her sister-ship *Jean Bart* made it to Casablanca in an even more unfinished condition. *Richelieu* sailed to Dakar, in Senegal, where other French units had gathered, and where the exiled fleet was later attacked by the British. Damaged but not irreparably, *Richelieu* and her crew finally managed to join up with the Allies and sail to the USA for a major refit (*Jean Bart* ended up in Vichy French hands). This work was completed in 1943, and added new radar and much expanded AA armament. From then on *Richelieu* sailed with the British Far Eastern Fleet. In 1946 she was formally handed back to French control after undertaking some sailing around former French colonies in Indo-China. In 1956 *Richelieu* was transferred into the reserve and ended her days as an accommodation ship in Brest harbour before being broken up in 1964.

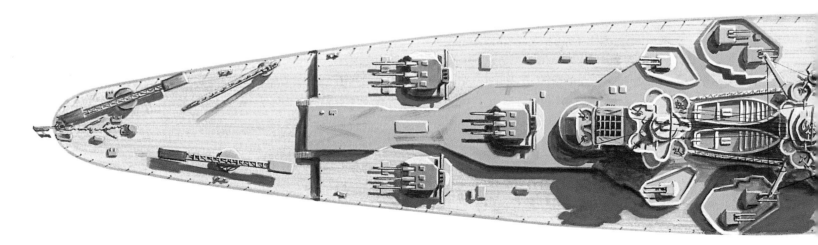

Battleships and Battlecruisers

Specification

Displacement:	35,000t standard; 43,293t deep load
Dimensions:	length (overall) 813ft 2in (247.85m); beam (at the waterline) 108ft 3in (32.99m); draught 31ft 7in (9.63m)
Machinery:	six Indret boilers driving four-shaft Parson geared turbines, developing 150,000hp
Maximum speed:	32kt
Armour:	belt 13.5in to 9.75in (343mm to 248mm); main deck 6.75in to 6in (171mm to 152mm); main turrets 17.5in to 6.75in (44mm to 171mm); secondary turrets 5.5in to 2.75in (140mm to 70mm)
Armament:	eight 15in (381mm) main guns, nine 6in (152mm) secondary guns, 12 3.9in (99mm) AA guns, eight 37mm AA guns (replaced by 56 40mm AA guns), 16 13.2mm AA guns (replaced by 48 20mm AA guns), plus three aircraft
Complement:	1670
Country:	France

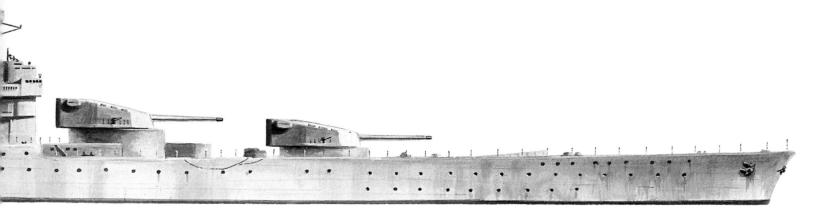

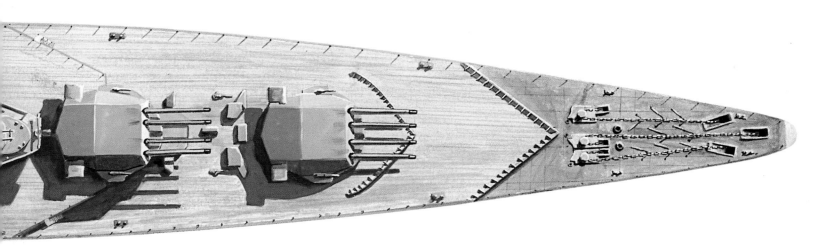

HMS *Rodney*

HMS *Rodney* was the second and final member of the *Nelson*-class battleships, the first British capital ships to be built under the terms of the Washington Treaty. For battleships the most important stipulations of this treaty were those that set maximum displacement at 35,000 tons and gun calibre at 16in (406mm). The Admiralty already had plans for its 1921 'G3' battlecruisers in their final stages, but these ships exceeded the Washington limits. It was decided, therefore, to build a cut-down version of the 'G3', using the same main guns but reducing the heavy armour coverage dramatically. This need to economise on armour was the main reason behind the decision to concentrate all the main turrets forward, within the same (single) armoured section. The *Nelson* class became the first British battleships to have 16in (406mm) guns and triple turrets. For the first time also the secondary armament was mounted in powered turrets. The positioning of the main guns was not ideal. Their blast effect was so strong that they were effectively limited to firing in a 180° arc

forward, for fear of damaging the ship. The guns themselves also proved troublesome and suffered from a poor rate of fire, though this problem was remedied by the early stages of World War II. As the years passed it also became clear that the armour protection which was once impressive, though limited, was increasingly vulnerable to air attack. HMS *Rodney* was laid down on 28 December 1922 (the same day as HMS *Nelson*), launched on 17 December 1925 and completed in November 1927. *Rodney* was fitted with an aircraft catapult above its centre 'X' turret, but this was removed between 1942 and 1943. Both *Rodney* and *Nelson* fought a successful war and *Rodney* is best known for her role in the hunt for the *Bismarck*. Along with HMS *King George V, Rodney* played a major part in sinking the German warship. Her service included providing part of the heavy naval firepower needed to protect the vital Malta resupply convoy of August 1942. By war's end, however, the *Nelson*s were showing their age and both ships were broken up in 1948.

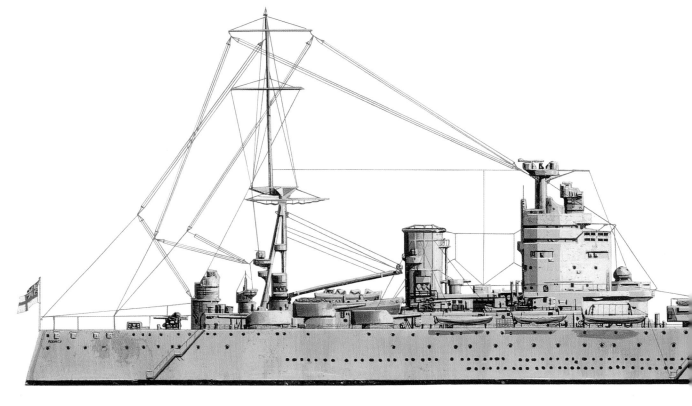

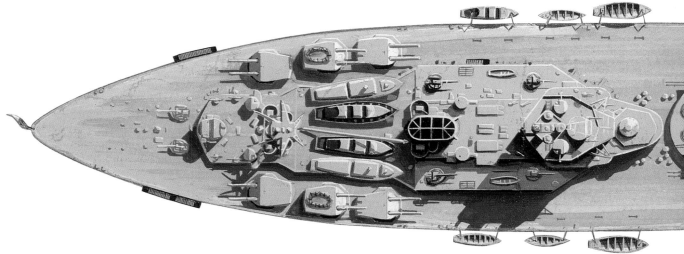

Battleships and Battlecruisers

Specification

Displacement:	33,730t standard; 43,150t deep load
Dimensions:	length (overall) 710ft (216.4m); beam (at the waterline) 106ft (32.3m); draught 28ft 1in (8.56m)
Machinery:	eight Admiralty three-drum boilers driving two-shaft Brown and Curtis geared turbines, developing 45,000hp
Maximum speed:	23kt
Armour:	belt 14in to 13in (356mm to 330mm); bulkheads 12in to 14in (305mm to 356mm); main turrets 16in to 7.25in (406mm to 184mm); secondary turrets 15in to 12in (381mm to 305mm)
Armament:	nine 16in (406mm) main guns, 12 6in (152mm) secondary guns, six 4.7in (119mm) guns, eight two-pounder 'pom pom' AA guns, 60/70 20mm Oerlikon AA guns, two 24.5in (621mm) torpedo tubes, plus two aircraft
Country:	GB
Complement:	1314

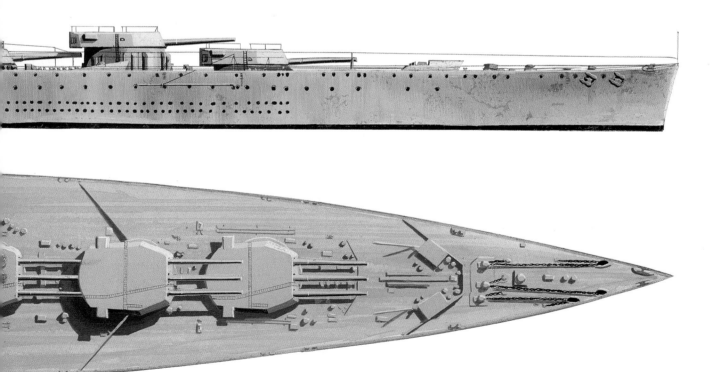

HMS *Royal Oak*

The *Royal Sovereign-* (or *Revenge-*) class battleships were the best available to the Royal Navy before the outbreak of World War I. HMS *Royal Oak* was a 1914-vintage battleship and a veteran of that war. These ships were developed from the historic *Iron Duke* class and armed with highly accurate 15in (381mm) guns. Good armour protection was fitted, particularly underwater bulkheads and torpedo defences. The *Royal Sovereign*s were designed with oil-burning engines, but in fear of wartime fuel shortages, plans were made to convert them to coal-fired boilers. This was halted by the intervention of Admiral Fisher, the First Sea Lord, and the ships retained their original engines which also had a speed advantage. They were not as fast as the rival *Queen Elizabeth* class, but they were much steadier gun platforms. HMS *Royal Oak* was launched on 17 November 1914, and in the mid-1920s she was refitted with a bulged hull, increased draught and a greater deep load. Between 1934 and 1936 additional armour was fitted over the magazines and engine rooms. It was the only ship in its class to be so modified. At the outbreak of World War II *Royal Oak* was a capable but ageing battleship. However, she never got a chance to prove herself in action. On the night of 13 October 1939, the German U-boat captain Lieutenant Commander Gunther Prien penetrated Scapa Flow, the anchorage that sheltered the British Home Fleet and which had always been thought to be impenetrable. Using the cover of the Northern Lights, Prien took his submarine *U-47* up the channel until he was in range of the British battleships. HMS *Royal Oak* was sunk by three torpedoes and HMS *Resolution* and HMS *Ramillies* were both damaged. Prien escaped and was highly decorated for his daring action. The attack was a severe blow to British morale and prestige in the early days of the war.

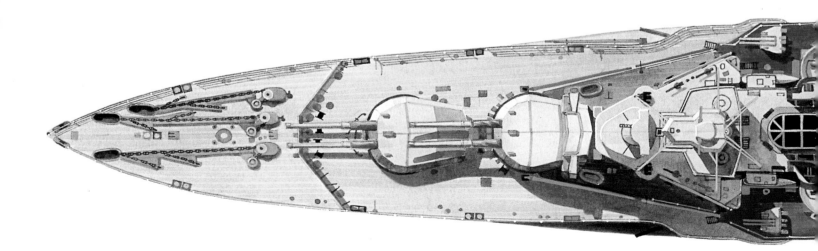

Battleships and Battlecruisers

Specification

Displacement: 28,000t standard; 31,200t deep load

Dimensions: length (overall) 624ft 3in (190.27m); beam (at the waterline) 88ft 6in (26.97m); draught 28ft 7in (8.71m)

Machinery: 18 Babcock & Wilcox boilers driving four Parsons turbines, developing 42,650hp

Maximum speed: 22kt

Armour: belt 13in to 4in (330mm to 102mm); bulkheads 4in to 1in (102mm to 25mm); main turrets 13in to 4.5in (330mm to 115mm); secondary turrets 6in (152mm)

Armament: eight 15in (381mm) main guns, 14 6in (152mm) secondary guns, two 3in (75mm) guns, four three-pounder guns, four 21in (533mm) torpedo tubes

Complement: 997

Country: GB

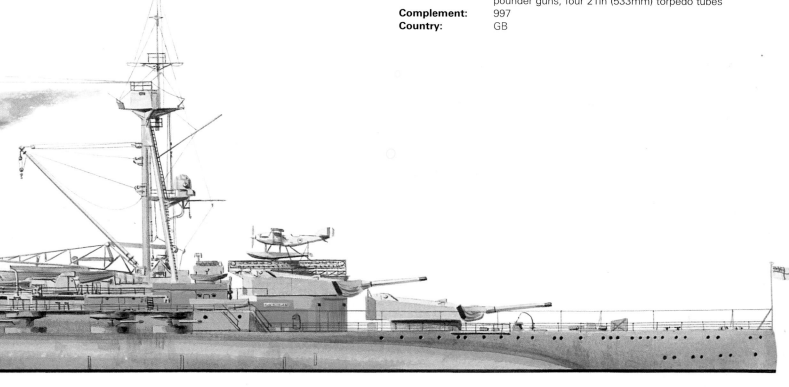

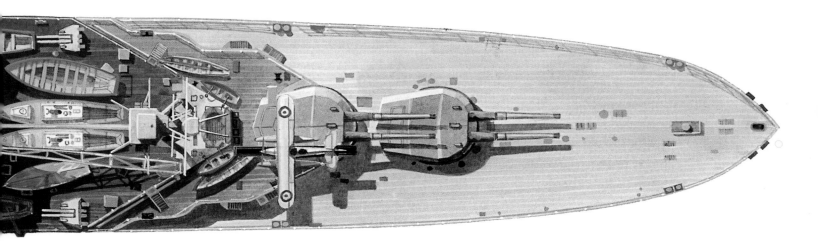

HMS *Warspite*

The *Queen Elizabeth* class was the yardstick against which other World War I battleships were measured, and it was the first of its kind to be built with oil-fired boilers. HMS *Warspite* was the second of the class to be built and like all the others (except HMS *Queen Elizabeth* herself) she was a veteran of the Battle of Jutland, which did so much to shape later warship designs. At Jutland HMS *Warspite* was badly damaged, but she survived. The *Queen Elizabeth*s were armed with 15in (381mm) guns at a time when rival vessels were just being introduced with 14in (356mm) guns. The battleships were well protected, as their oil-fired boilers saved weight that could be given over to armour plating. During World War I the *Queen Elizabeth*s acted together as a distinct fast battleship squadron. After the war they remained among the best ships in the fleet, and during the 1920s they were extensively modernised. HMS *Warspite* underwent a refit between 1924 and 1926 which involved adding new light guns, trunking the two original funnels into one single unit, and fitting side bulges for added underwater protection. Between 1934 and 1936 a second phase of modernisation was initiated, this time adding increased armour on the middle deck over the magazines and engine rooms. New AA guns were added and a cross-deck catapult with provision for four aircraft was also fitted (the catapult was later removed in 1943). During World War II all the *Queen Elizabeth*s played important roles, though HMS *Barham* was torpedoed by *U-331* in 1941. HMS *Warspite* endured a long war and was involved in the Norwegian campaign, the Battle of Atlantic, and combat in the Indian Ocean. She also provided fire support for the Allied landings in Sicily. While operational in the Mediterranean, on 16 September 1943, *Warspite* was attacked by German bombers and sustained heavy damage from FX1400 'Fritz-X' guided missiles, taking on 5000 tons of water and barely making it back to Malta. Only temporary repairs were made and she was used as a patched-up bombardment ship with only six operational 15in (381mm) guns, and no 6in (152mm) guns or other light armament. *Warspite* provided fire support for the D-Day Normandy landings, and was damaged again by a mine on 13 June 1944, but survived the rest of the war to be sold off in 1946. Over her years of service from 1916 to 1945, HMS *Warspite* sustained the most battle damage of any British warship.

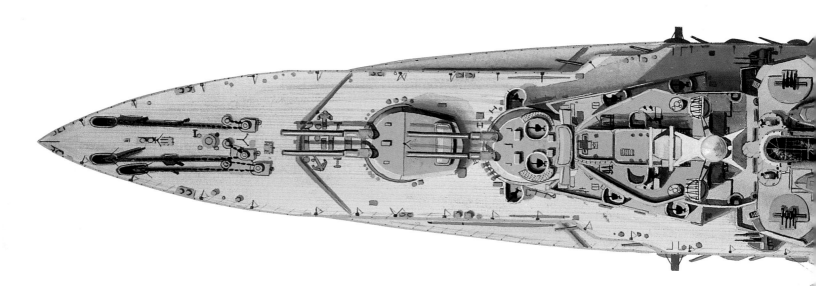

Battleships and Battlecruisers

Specification (after 1936)

Displacement: 27,500t standard; 36,450t deep load
Dimensions: length (overall) 646ft 1in (196.9m); beam (at the waterline) 90ft 6in (27.6m); draught 33ft 1in (10.08m)
Machinery: 18 Admiralty three-drum boilers driving four-shaft Parsons geared turbines, developing 80,000hp
Maximum speed: 23.5kt
Armour: belt 13in to 4in (330mm to 102mm); bulkheads 6in to 4in (152mm to 102mm); main turrets 13in to 5in (330mm to 127mm); secondary turrets 6in (152mm)
Armament: eight 15in (381mm) main guns, eight 6in (152mm) secondary guns, eight 4in (102mm) quick-firing guns, 32 two-pounder 'pom pom' AA guns (later 40 'pom poms' and 35 20mm AA guns)
Complement: 925
Country: GB

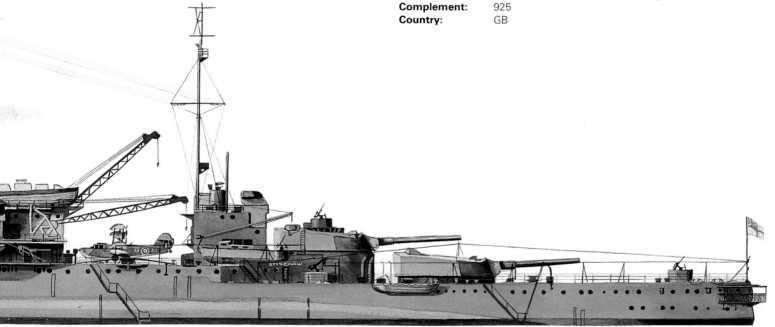

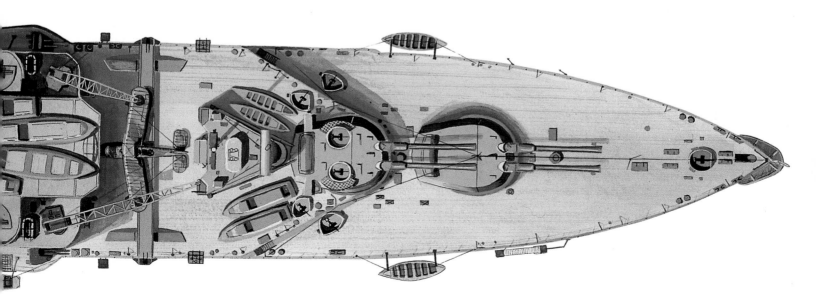

Yamato

Under conditions of great secrecy in 1937, Japan laid down the first of four planned super-battleships, designed to outgun the best ships in the US Navy. These immense vessels had the greatest displacement, the heaviest armour and the largest guns of any battleships in the history of naval warfare. The lead ship in the class was the *Yamato*. Armed with huge 18in (457mm) guns, in triple turrets, *Yamato* had an effective range of 45,960yds (42,000m), with 3220lb (1460kg) shells, and could fire at a rate of one-and-a-half to two rounds per minute. In turn, she was designed to resist hits from 18in (457mm) shells fired from 22,000 to 33,000yds (20,100 to 30,170m). Protection against bombs was equally impressive, though in contrast submarine protection seemed surprisingly lacking, but once in combat this did not prove to be the case. *Yamato* was laid down on 4 November 1937, launched on 8 July 1940 and completed on 16 December 1941. She was followed by a second super-battleship *Musashi* in 1942. A third vessel, *Shinano*, was converted into an aircraft carrier as

the needs of the war changed. The intended fourth ship was never completed. Once afloat the *Yamato*s were perhaps the most sleek and elegant warships ever built, but by the time they were at sea, Japan was already beginning to lose its grip on the Pacific. Without their own effective air cover the *Yamato*s were vulnerable to attack from US aircraft carriers and as a result the Japanese command proved reluctant to deploy the super-battleships. Both vessels, the most highly prized targets in the Japanese navy, were finally caught and sunk, though not without some difficulty. *Musashi* absorbed perhaps 19 torpedo strikes and 17 direct bomb hits before sinking at Leyte Gulf in October 1944. *Yamato* remained operational for longer but she was finally intercepted on 7 April 1945, in the East China Sea, while making a suicidal dash to relieve besieged Japanese forces on Okinawa. A force of no less than 386 US Navy aircraft was committed to sinking the *Yamato*, which they did, but only after 11 to 15 torpedo hits and a further seven bomb hits.

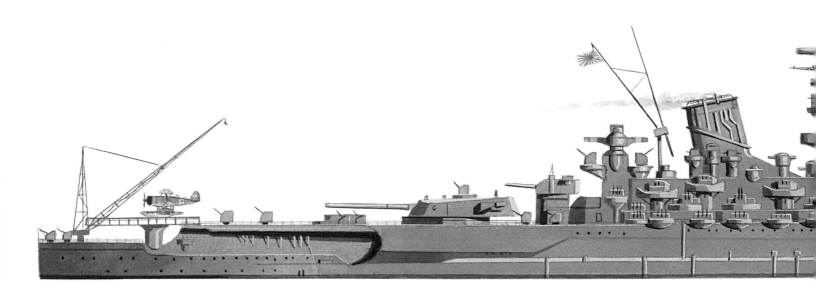

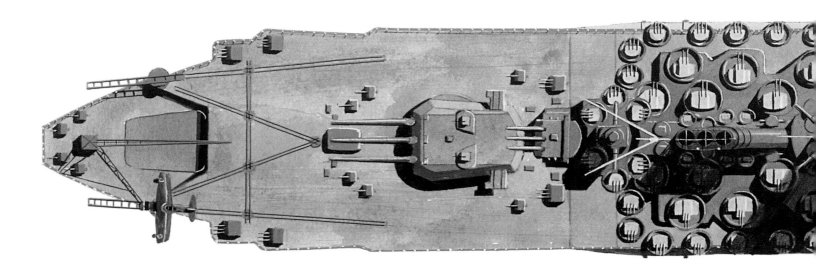

Battleships and Battlecruisers

Specification

Displacement:	63,000t standard; 71,659t deep load
Dimensions:	length (overall) 862ft 9in (262.9m); beam (at the waterline) 121ft 1in (36.9m); draught 34ft 1in (10.39m)
Machinery:	12 boilers driving four-shaft geared turbines, developing 150,000hp
Maximum speed:	27kt
Armour:	belt 16.1in (40.89cm); deck 9.1in to 7in (231mm to 178mm); bulkheads 6in to 4in (152mm to 102mm); main turrets 25.6in to 7.6in (643mm to 193mm)
Armament:	nine 18.1in (460mm) main guns, 12 6.1in (155mm) secondary guns, replaced by 12 5in (127mm) guns, 12 5in (127mm) dual-purpose guns, 150 25mm AA guns (by 1945), four 13.2mm AA guns, plus seven aircraft
Complement:	2500
Country:	Japan

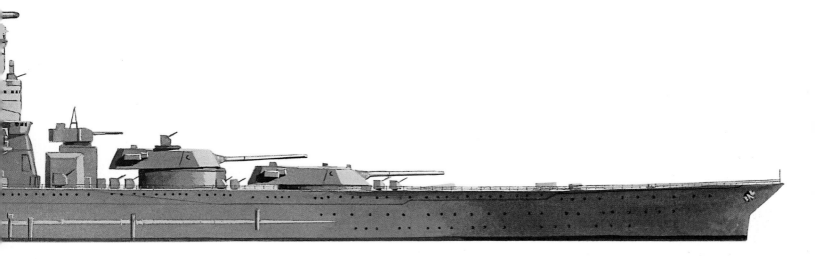

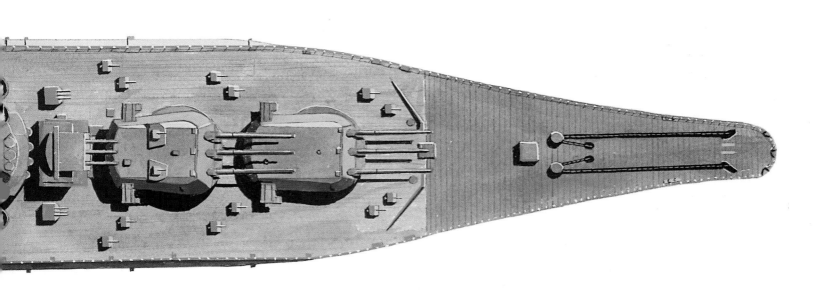

Chokai

Japan's *Takao*-class cruisers were based on the earlier *Nachi* class, the first heavy cruisers to be ordered in accordance with the 1922 Washington Treaty limitations. These ships were slightly heavier than the 10,000 tons allowed, and the *Takao*s were heavier still, with an actual displacement of 11,400 tons. The stated figure was 9850 tons. Together with the four *Nachi*- and two *Aoba*-class ships, the four *Takao*-class vessels formed the backbone of Japan's modern heavy cruiser fleet at the beginning of the war. Improvements incorporated into the *Takao*s included bridge armour on a revised structure, an upright second funnel and modified torpedo tubes that could be swung out to fire. The main guns could be elevated by up to 70° for anti-aircraft duties. *Chokai* was laid down on 26 March 1928, launched on 5 April 1931 and completed on 30 June 1932. Just prior to the outbreak

of World War II, *Chokai* underwent modernisation that replaced her original 4.7in (119mm) secondary guns with 5in (127mm) guns and added new 13.2mm AA guns. Of the four *Takao*-class cruisers, three were sunk in the Leyte Gulf battles of 1944, the engagement that wiped out the last elements of the Japanese surface fleet. Both *Atago* and *Maya* (the second and third ships in the class) were sunk on 23 October 1944 and *Chokai* was sunk just two days later on 25 October. *Chokai* was attached to Vice Admiral Kurito's main Centre Force at Leyte, and was one of the 10 heavy cruisers that took part in the Battle of Samar. She was sunk after repeated dive bombing attacks, having been damaged by the tiny US destroyer group that held off the far superior Japanese force.

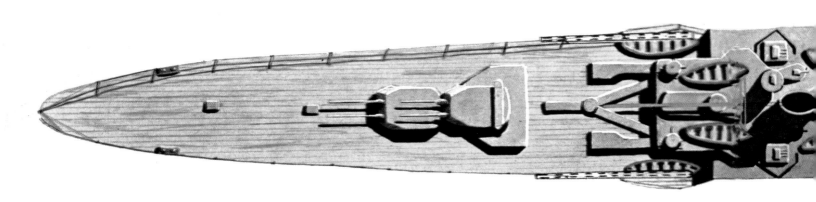

Specification

Displacement:	13,400t standard; 14,600t deep load
Dimensions:	length (overall) 668ft 6in (203.75m); beam (at the waterline) 59ft 2in (18m); draught 20ft 1in (6.12m)
Machinery:	12 boilers driving four-shaft geared turbines, developing 130,000hp
Maximum speed:	35.5kt
Armour:	belt 4.9 to 3.9in (12.45 to 9.9cm); deck 1.4in (35mm); main turrets 1in (25mm)
Armament:	10 8in (203mm) main guns, four 4.7in (119mm) AA guns, replaced by eight 5in (127mm) AA guns, four 40mm AA guns, four 13.2mm AA guns, eight 24in (609mm) torpedo tubes, plus three aircraft
Complement:	773
Country:	Japan

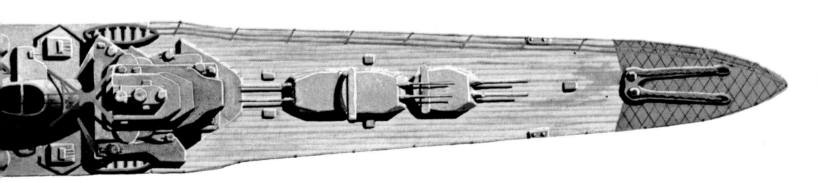

HMS *Exeter*

HMS *Exeter* was the sole ship of her class, a cruiser that followed the lead set by the earlier *York, Norfolk* and *London* classes. As such she was a small, lightly armoured vessel with 8in (203mm) guns. *Exeter* featured modern innovations such as shipborne aircraft, but her own guns could not be elevated beyond 50°, which limited their effectiveness against enemy aircraft. *Exeter* was laid down in 1 August 1928, launched on 18 July 1929 and completed on 23 July 1931. She remained unchanged throughout the 1930s until the outbreak of World War II. Once hostilities had commenced *Exeter* soon found herself in

action. Together with HMS *Achilles* and HMS *Ajax, Exeter* was part of the British cruiser squadron commanded by Commodore (later Admiral) H. H. Harwood that was involved in the famous action against the *Graf Spee* at the River Plate in December 1939. After engaging *Graf Spee* alone, *Exeter* was hit by seven 11in (280mm) shells from the German cruiser, and fragments from other near-misses. She was badly damaged, with all of her own 8in (203mm) guns knocked out. Repairs took 14 months, during which time her basic armament was overhauled and upgraded, and the main gun turrets given a 70° elevation. *Exeter*

Specification

Displacement:	8,390t standard; 11,000t deep load
Dimensions:	length (overall) 575ft (175.26m); beam (at the waterline) 58ft (17.68m); draught 20ft 3in (6.17m)
Machinery:	eight Admiralty three-drum boilers driving four-shaft Parsons geared turbines, developing 80,000hp
Maximum speed:	32kt
Armour:	box protection to ammunition storage 4 to 1in (10.16 to 2.54cm); side 3in (7.62cm)
Armament:	six 8in (203mm) main guns, four 4in (102mm) quick-firing guns (later eight), two two-pounder 'pom pom' AA guns, six 21in (533mm) torpedo tubes
Complement:	630
Country:	GB

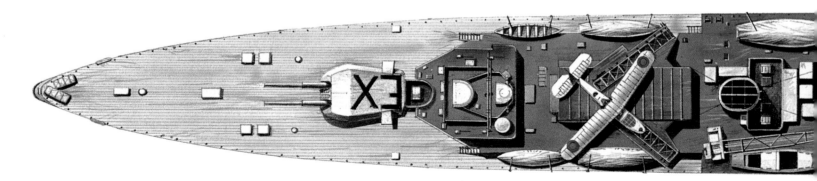

returned to the fleet, but in the Battle of the Java Sea, in February/March 1942, she was hit by a Japanese 8in (203mm) shell, which damaged the aft boiler room and cut her cruising speed to 16kt. Two days later, *Exeter* was again attacked by Japanese cruisers, this time sustaining hits to her forward boiler room. *Exeter* lost all power, was abandoned and scuttled. Before she sank of her own accord she was sunk by a torpedo fired by a Japanese destroyer on 1 March 1942.

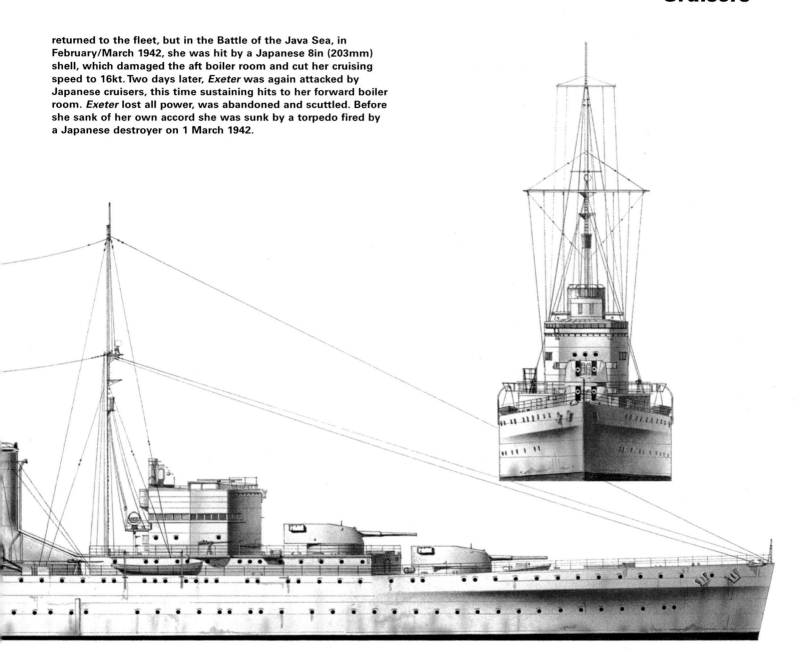

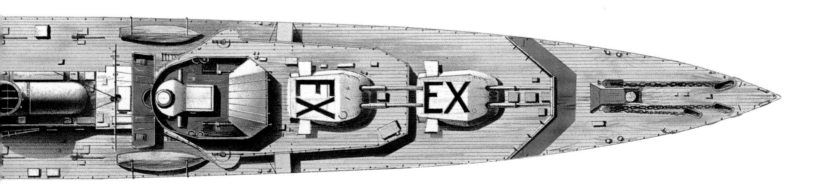

Giovanni Delle Bande Nere

Italy's naval designers showed flair in developing modern fighting ships to expand the navy in the late 1930s. The Italian navy fielded a series of cleverly engineered cruisers and battleships, though the quality of the ships was never reflected in their operational record. The *Giussano*-class were the first cruisers to be built in Italy after World War I. They were part of the major 1927–28 expansion programme and were conceived as fast scout cruisers, intended to hunt and sink smaller enemy ships, such as destroyers. What drove this particular strategy was the arrival on the scene of new large French destroyers such as the *Aigle, Lion* and *Jaguar* classes. Unfortunately for the Italian ships, too much was sacrificed for the sake of speed and they were very lightly armoured. So poor was their basic protection that a typical destroyer would be capable of inflicting serious damage once within range. Built for the easy conditions of the Mediterranean, the class was rather unstable and lacking in endurance. Crews also disliked the cramped conditions inside. Some of these flaws were corrected on the subsequent tranche of *Cardona*-class cruisers, which belonged to the same

Condottieri type as the *Giussano* class. The *Giussano*s certainly achieved their performance goals and, on trials, the lead ship *Albercio Da Barbiano* maintained nearly 40kt for eight hours, with a maximum speed of 42kt. *Giovanni Delle Bande Nere* was the fourth and final ship in the class. She was laid down on 31 October 1928, launched on 27 April 1930 and completed in April 1931. During her own sea trials she attained a maximum of 38.2kt, but regular sea speed was 30kt. All of the ships were equipped for minelaying and a catapult was located on the forecastle. The *Giussano* class fared badly at the hands of the Royal Navy and all were sunk by 1942. Two of the cruisers were sunk on the same day off Cape Bon by a group of four destroyers, underlining the poor design of the Italian armour. The third vessel was sunk by the cruiser HMS *Sydney*, and finally *Giovanni Delle Bande Nere* herself was torpedoed and sunk by the submarine HMS *Urgent* off Stromboli on 1 April 1942.

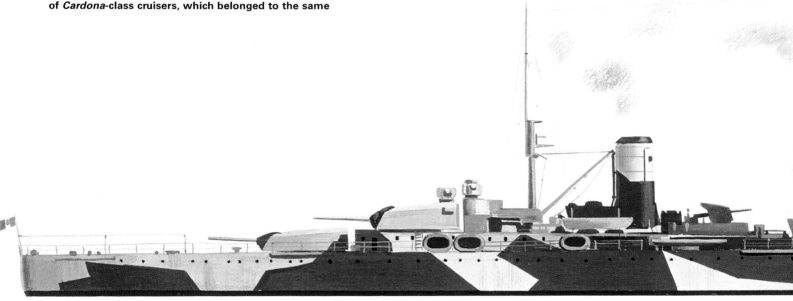

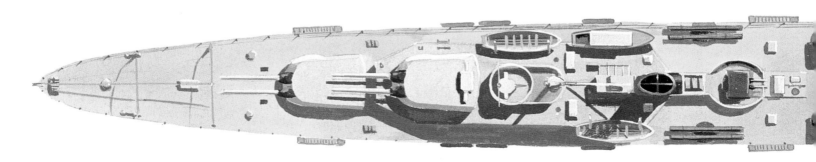

Specification

Displacement:	5130t standard; 6844t deep load
Dimensions:	length (overall) 555ft 5in (169.29m); beam (at the waterline) 50ft 10in (15.49m); draught 17ft 9in (5.4m)
Machinery:	six Yarrow boilers driving two-shaft Belluzzo geared turbines, developing 128,200hp
Maximum speed:	30kt (typical)
Armour:	belt 9.4in to 7in (240mm to 178mm); deck 7.9in (200mm); bulkheads 7.9in (200mm); main turrets 9in (229mm)
Armament:	eight 6in (152mm) main guns, six 4in (102mm) AA guns, eight 37mm AA guns, eight 13.2mm AA, four 21in (533mm) torpedo tubes, plus two aircraft
Complement:	1830 to 1950
Country:	Italy

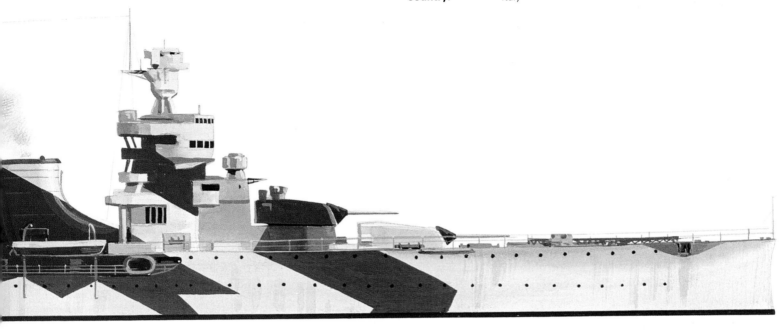

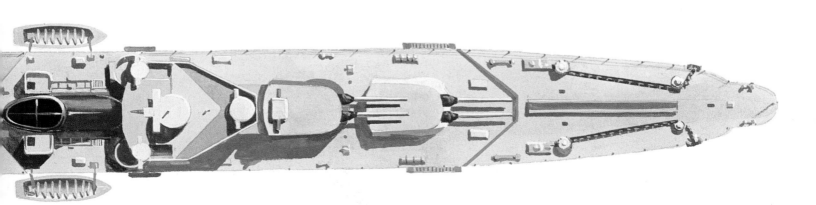

USS *Indianapolis* (CA-35)

Few ships hold such a place in naval history as the USS *Indianapolis*, or such a controversial one. She was the second and last of the *Portland*-class cruisers to be built, from an intended total of five. The subsequent ships were revised to offer better armour, as both *Portland* and *Indianapolis* were poorly protected from submarine attacks. *Indianapolis* was laid down on 31 March 1930, launched on 7 November 1931 and commissioned on 15 November 1932. She served as the flagship of the US Navy's Fifth Fleet, but *Indianapolis* has entered the public consciousness through the film *Jaws*, after the scene where the sharkhunter Quint (played by Robert Shaw) tells of the night she was lost and the fate of her crew. *Indianapolis* was the last major US ship to be sunk in World War II but also played an instrumental part in bringing the war to a close. She carried the first atomic bomb from the United States to the island of Tinian, where the B-29s of 509th Composite Group were preparing to drop it on Hiroshima. *Indianapolis* performed this vital mission safely and was then ordered to proceed from Tinian to the Philippines, where she would join the invasion fleet assembling at Leyte Gulf. It was on this journey that *Indianapolis* was torpedoed by the Japanese submarine, *I-58*. At 0014 hours on 30 July 1945, two torpedoes split the ship open and caused her to sink rapidly. Of the 1196 crew on board, about 900 made it into the water. When the sun rose the next day the survivors were attacked by sharks, attacks which continued for five days until rescue arrived. On the fourth day after the sinking, dinghies and wreckage were seen accidentally by a US Navy PV-1 Ventura, which reported 'many men in the water'. A PBY Catalina was dispatched and its pilot in turn alerted a US destroyer, the *Cecil Doyle*. The *Doyle*'s captain decided to divert to the rescue area

under his own authority. When the PBY arrived to drop rafts and supplies, the pilot could see men being attacked by sharks and disregarded his orders not to land in the water to pick up survivors. Only when men were dragged out of the water was the loss of the *Indianapolis* properly recognised. The PBY picked up 56 survivors, with some even tied to the wings, and stayed in position on the surface to await the arrival of the *Cecil Doyle*. The destroyer's searchlight was the first signal to many of the survivors that help had finally come. Of the 900 men who went into the water only 317 were rescued. What happened next stirred a controversy that rages to this day. The captain of the *Indianapolis* was court-martialled for the loss of his ship, the only US captain to face such a charge. Captain McVay had orders to maintain a zig-zag course to avoid interception, but on a cloudy night he opted to maintain a faster course straight ahead as the risk of detection was so low. Just after midnight the clouds

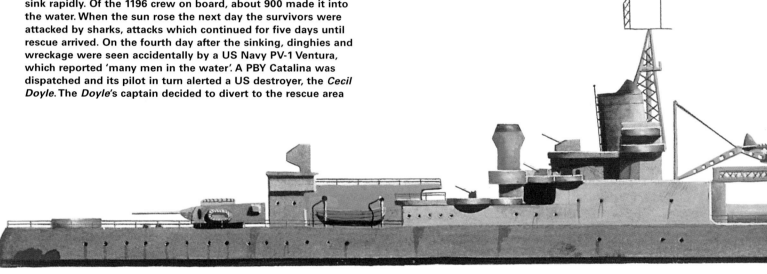

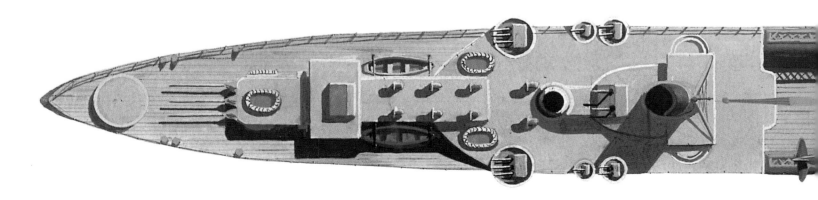

cleared long enough for the captain of the *I-58*, Mochitura Hashimoto, to see *Indianapolis* and fire at her. Hashimoto was brought to the court martial by the US Navy, and he testified that he would have hit the cruiser whether she was zig-zagging or not. Nevertheless, the authorities deemed that McVay had disobeyed his orders and he was disgraced. Since then it has emerged that the US Navy knew that a Japanese submarine was active in the area (*I-58* having sunk another ship four days earlier) but did not inform McVay. *Indianapolis* had requested an anti-submarine escort but was denied one. The US had broken the Japanese naval codes and intercepted the message from *I-58* reporting the loss of the cruiser, but did not act on it. Nor was a search launched when *Indianapolis* failed to arrive on schedule. In the light of this evidence a campaign is still being run to revoke the prosecution of Captain McVay.

Specification

Displacement:	10,258t standard; 12,755t deep load
Dimensions	length (overall) 610ft (185.92m); beam (at the waterline) 66ft (20.1m); draught 21ft (6.4m)
Machinery:	eight Yarrow boilers driving four-shaft Parsons turbines, developing 107,000hp
Maximum speed:	32.5kt
Armour:	belt 5.57in to 2.25in (146mm to 57mm)
Armament:	nine 8in (203mm) main guns, eight 5in (127mm) secondary guns, 40mm and 20mm AA guns, eight 12.7mm machine guns, plus four aircraft
Complement:	917
Country:	USA

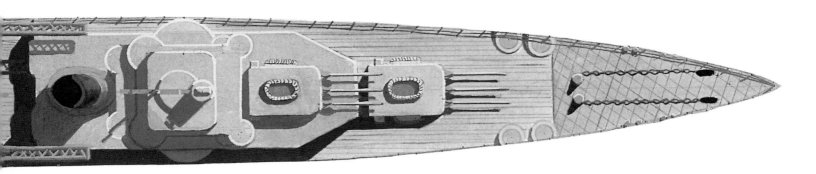

HMS *Jamaica*

The *Fiji*-class cruisers were considered to be the best available to the Royal Navy in the early years of the war. All 11 ships were named after British possessions or overseas territories. The class was hurriedly laid down between 1938 and 1939 and entered service from early 1941 onwards. They were mostly armed with 12 6in (152mm) guns (though some carried only nine), had appropriate armour and could exceed 30kt. HMS *Jamaica* was the sixth ship to be laid down, on 28 April 1939. She was launched on 16 November 1940 and completed on 29 June 1942. By then several of her sister-ships had seen considerable action, and HMS *Fiji* herself had been sunk. Despite fighting a number of heavy engagements and

sustaining serious damage in some cases, the other 10 *Fiji*-class cruisers all survived the war. HMS *Jamaica* is best known for her clashes with larger German warships. While serving as part of Convoy 51B to Murmansk, *Jamaica* encountered the German raiders *Lützow* and *Admiral Hipper*. The *Jamaica* scored direct hits on the *Hipper* causing damage to her boiler room before contact was broken. Later, in the company of the battleship HMS *Duke of York* and the cruiser HMS *Belfast,* the *Jamaica* participated in the sinking of the *Scharnhorst* on 26 December 1943, effectively ending the role of the German surface high seas fleet. *Jamaica* continued to serve into the 1950s, but was finally broken up in 1960.

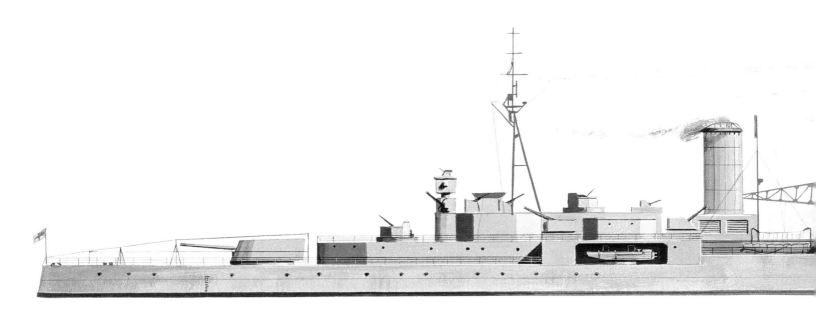

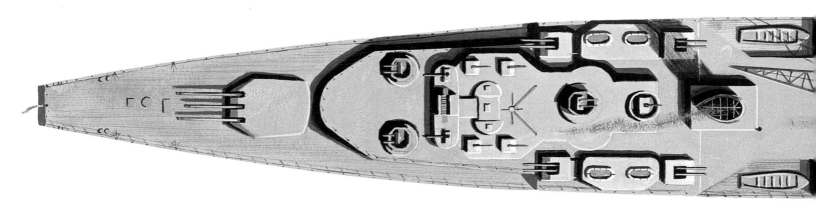

Specification

Displacement:	8530t standard; 11,450t deep load
Dimensions:	length (overall) 555ft 6in (169.3m); beam (at the waterline) 62ft (18.9m); draught 20ft 9in (6.32m)
Machinery:	eight Admiralty three-drum boilers driving four-shaft Parsons geared turbines, developing 72,500hp
Maximum speed:	31.5kt
Armour:	belt 3.5in to 3.25in (89mm to 81mm); bulkheads 2in to 1.5in (50mm to 38mm); turrets 2in to 1in (50mm to 25mm)
Armament:	12 6in (152mm) main guns, eight 4in (102mm) quick-firing guns, eight two-pounder 'pom pom' AA guns (later increased), two 40mm Bofors AA guns, six 21in (533mm) torpedo tubes, and two aircraft
Complement:	920
Country:	GB

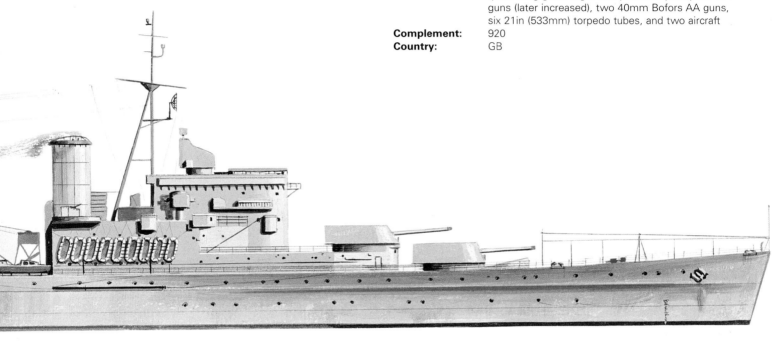

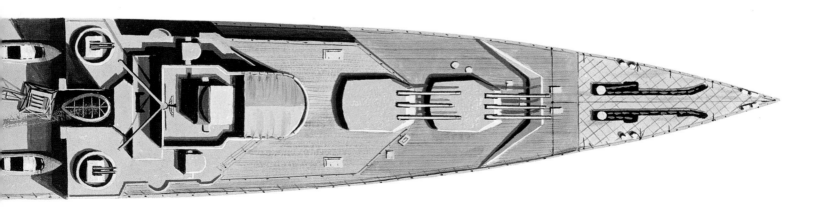

Köln

The Kriegsmarine's three *K*-class cruisers were the public face of the resurgent German navy during the 1930s. They were a bold new design that used modern techniques such as electric welding in their construction. For the first time a combination of steam and diesel powerplants was fitted, though the two could only function separately. This still allowed for a diesel cruising speed of 10kt and a turbine dash of 32kt. The nine 6in (152mm) main guns were fitted in three triple turrets. The two rear turrets were positioned offset to the centreline and could fire at 40° elevation in all directions. *Königsberg* was the lead ship, launched in 1927, followed by *Karlsruhe*, later the same year. The *Köln* was laid down on 7 August 1926, launched on 23 May 1928 and commissioned on 15 January 1930. Before the war the three cruisers were invaluable as training vessels and they each made several 'friendly' round-the-world cruises. Once the war had started it was no longer plain sailing for the *K* class. Both *Königsberg* and *Karlsruhe* were diverted from mine-laying duties in the Atlantic to participate in the invasion of Norway, as part of the ill-fated Task Forces 3 and 4. Both were so badly damaged – on 10 and 9 April 1940 respectively – that they were put out of action for the rest of the war. *Köln* had joined *Königsberg* as part of Task Force 3, but managed to escape the devastation wrought among the German ships. From 1940 until 1943 she remained within the Baltic Sea or in Norway, along with the bulk of Germany's remaining surface navy, part of Hitler's misguided 'force in waiting'. In 1944 she became a training ship, still in the Baltic, and escorted convoys to and from Norway. On 3 March 1945 she was caught undergoing work at the Wilhelmshaven ship yards by an RAF bombing raid and was sunk at the dockside. She was decommissioned in April, though her guns were used for a local battery. The wreck of the *Köln* was finally scrapped in 1946.

Specification

Displacement:	6500t standard; 8130t full load
Dimensions:	length (overall) 570ft 10in (174m); beam (at the waterline) 50ft 2in (15.29m); draught 18ft 3in (5.56m)
Machinery:	six navy boilers plus two double-acting four-stroke 10-cylinder MAN diesel engines, driving two-shaft navy geared turbines, developing 1800hp (diesels) and 65,000hp (turbines)
Maximum speed:	32kt (10kt diesels only)
Armour:	belt 2.75in to 2in (70mm to 50mm); torpedo bulkhead 0.5in (12mm); turrets 1.25in (31mm)
Armament:	nine 6in (152mm) main guns, four 88mm guns, eight 37mm guns, eight 20mm AA guns, eight 19.5in (500mm) torpedo tubes, plus two aircraft
Complement:	850
Country:	Germany

HMS *Penelope*

With the *Arethusa* class, the Royal Navy tried to build the smallest possible useful cruiser. It was similar in design to the cruisers of the *Perth* class, but had only three turrets, instead of four. One unfortunate element of the design was that the magazines for the secondary 4in (102mm) guns were not near the guns themselves, which proved a serious problem in combat. The four *Arethusa*s were initially fitted with catapults and aircraft, but these were removed between 1940 and 1941. HMS *Penelope* was the third to be built. She was laid down on 30 May 1934, launched on 15 October 1935 and completed on 13 November 1936. The lightly armoured *Arethusa*s were not ideal vessels but they gave good service in the European theatres. Two

were sunk and two survived the war. HMS *Penelope* distinguished herself as one of the escorts involved in the infamous Force H convoy to Malta in 1942. With the battered island about to succumb to Axis air attacks, a last-ditch effort was made to force supplies through the German and Italian blockade. After intense air and sea battles only one merchant vessel made it to Malta, the US tanker *Ohio*, which was by then barely afloat. Her arrival was enough to keep Malta fighting. *Penelope* continued to serve with the Mediterranean and Home Fleets until 1944, when she was sunk on 18 February by the *U-410*. While steaming at 26kt *Penelope* was hit by first one and then a second torpedo, and sank straight away.

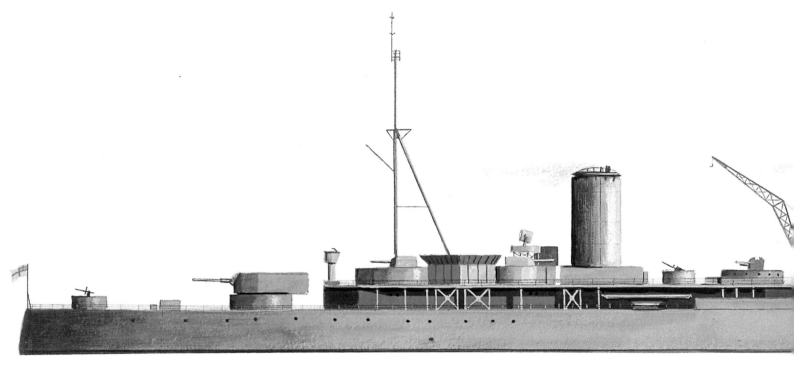

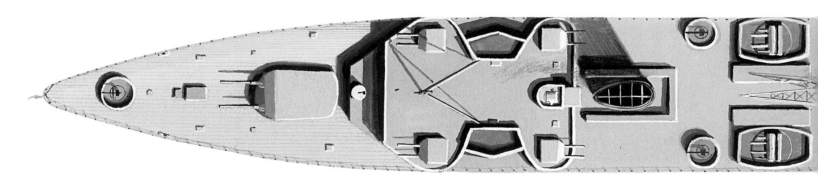

Specification

Displacement:	5270t standard; 6715t deep load
Dimensions:	length (overall) 506ft (154.23m); beam (at the waterline) 51ft (15.54m); draught 16ft 6in (5.03m)
Machinery:	four Admiralty three-drum boilers, driving four-shaft Parsons geared turbines, developing 64,000hp
Maximum speed:	32.3kt
Armour:	box protection to ammunition storage 3in to 1in (76mm to 25mm); belt 2.25in (57mm); bulkheads 1in (25mm); turrets 1in (25mm)
Armament:	six 6in (152mm) main guns, eight 4in (102mm) quick-firing guns, six 21in (533mm) torpedo tubes, and one aircraft (originally)
Complement:	500
Country:	GB

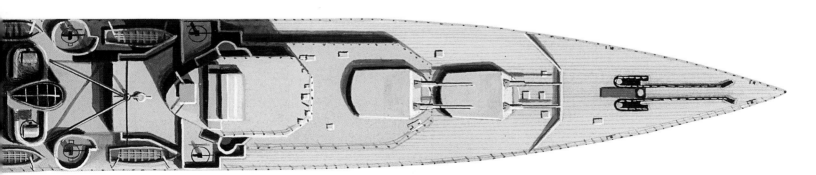

USS *Pensacola* (CA-24)

The two heavy cruisers of the *Pensacola* class were the first to be laid down in the US as 'treaty cruisers' – a reference to the 10,000-ton limitation placed on such warships by the 1922 Washington Treaty. The USS *Pensacola* was geared towards firepower and armed with 8in (203mm) guns when most rival cruisers had only 6in (152mm) guns. However, as combat ranges increased thanks to the introduction of accurate fire-direction techniques, the *Pensacola*s found themselves in danger of being outgunned by larger Japanese cruisers, and without sufficient armour to feel safe. Some security did come from the layout of the fire and engine rooms, which alternated through the ship, and thus were more likely to survive single shell or torpedo hits. The USS *Pensacola* was laid down on 27 October 1926, launched on 25 April 1929 and commissioned on 6 February 1930. She spent her pre-war years in the Atlantic and Pacific fleets, and was en route to Manila with a convoy from Pearl Harbor, when Pearl

Harbor was attacked by the Japanese. By February 1942, *Pensacola* was operating as part of Task Force 11 with the carrier *Lexington*. She provided AA protection for the *Lexington* against waves of Japanese bombers during the fighting off Bougainville, in the Solomons. *Pensacola* continued duty as a carrier escort in the Coral Sea, New Caledonia, and at the Battle of Midway. At Midway she escorted *Enterprise* and defended the stricken carrier *Yorktown*, preventing her from being attacked by Japanese torpedo bombers. She supported the recapture of Guadalcanal and rescued the survivors from the carrier *Hornet*, sunk during

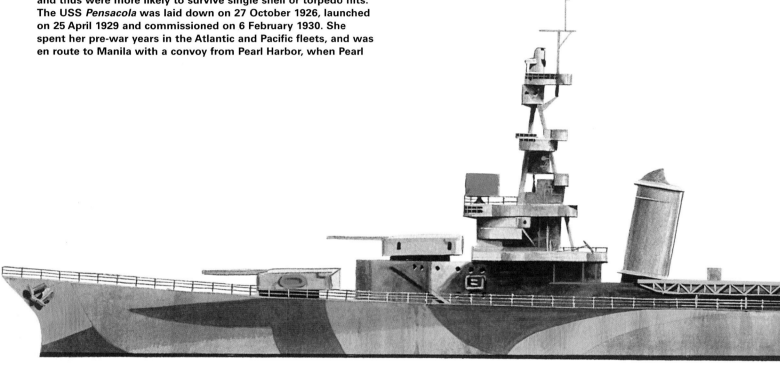

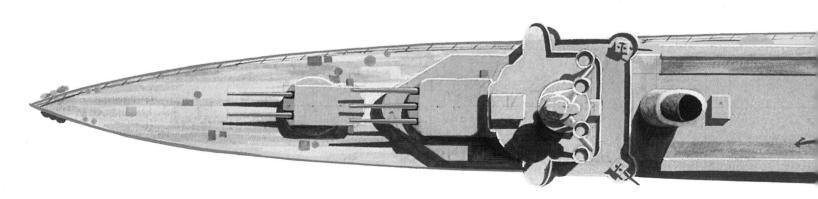

the battle of the Santa Cruz Islands. *Pensacola* fought in the Battle of Tassafaronga, at 'Ironbottom Sound' in November 1942. There she was torpedoed by a Japanese submarine but remained afloat and made it to harbour. In November 1943 she was back in action, shelling the islands of Betio and Tarawa and supporting the overall campaign in the Gilbert Islands. By January 1944, she was active in the Marshall Islands, and then sailed to Alaskan waters to attack the Kuriles in June. *Pensacola* was there for the invasion of the Philippines in October 1944, and the attack on Iwo Jima in February 1945. On 16 February, she was hit by a Japanese shore battery, but after repairs she took part in the assault on Okinawa, the final stepping stone before the invasion of Japan. This was her last action of World War II. *Pensacola* was used as a target ship in the Crossroads atomic tests of 1946, but she survived and was not finally expended until 1948.

Specification

Displacement:	9097t standard; 11,512t deep load
Dimensions:	length (overall) 585ft 8in (178.5m); beam (at the waterline) 65ft 3in (19.88m); draught 19ft 6in (5.94m)
Machinery:	eight White-Forster boilers, driving four-shaft Parsons turbines, developing 107,000hp
Maximum speed:	32.5kt
Armour:	belt 4in to 1in (102mm to 25mm)
Armament:	10 8in (203mm) main guns, four 5in (127mm) secondary guns, six quadruple 40mm AA guns, 20 twin 20mm AA guns, six 21in (533mm) torpedo tubes, plus four aircraft
Complement:	631

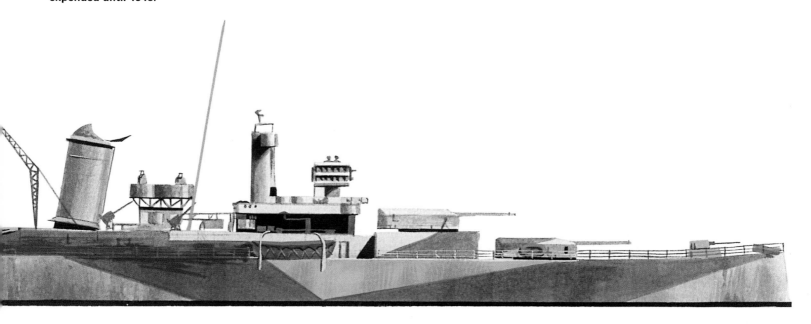

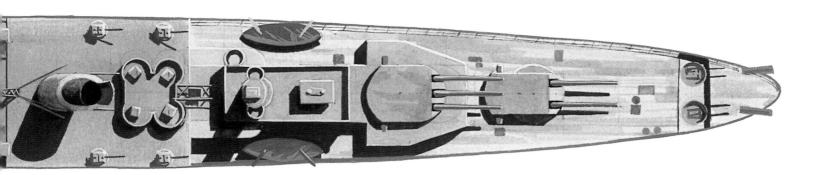

Pola

The Italian *Zara*-class cruisers followed a different path from other contemporary Italian designs, opting for armour rather than speed. It proved impossible, however, to accommodate the desired 8in (203mm) guns and armour within the limits of the Washington Treaty, so the limits were quietly ignored. Some attempt was made to stay within the 10,000-ton restriction, by fitting lightweight machinery and less armour in specific areas, but the ships were still overweight by about 1500 tons. The four *Zara*-class cruisers were built in two batches, with the *Pola* coming in the second. The ships were originally classified as light cruisers, then armoured cruisers (to distinguish them from other less well-protected ships) and finally as heavy cruisers. Despite their weight the cruisers were still fast, with a maximum speed of 35kt being achieved in special trials. *Pola* was laid down on 17 March 1929, launched on 27 April 1930 and completed on 20 October 1931. She was different to the other ships, being fitted with an enlarged bridge structure and lacking the distinctive flutes that ran along the forecastle sideplating on the other *Zara*s. During the late 1930s, the cruisers were modified to carry additional small calibre AA guns, replacing other larger guns, and more were steadily added as the war progressed. Like the rest of the Italian cruiser force, the *Zara*s did not fare well, and all four vessels were sunk, including three on the same day in 1941. On 29 March 1941, *Pola* was sailing as part of an Italian cruiser squadron that was engaged by the Royal Navy's Mediterranean Fleet, at the Battle of Matapan: the 'engagement' was in fact a carefully laid British trap. During this encounter *Pola* suffered heavy damage from an air-launched torpedo and was finally sunk by a British destroyer. Her two sister-ships, *Zara* and *Fiume*, sent to *Pola*'s aid, were then destroyed by gunfire.

Cruisers

Specification

Displacement:	11,545t standard; 14,330t deep load
Dimensions:	length (overall) 557ft 2in (169.8m); beam (at the waterline) 62ft 10in (19.15m); draught 21ft 11in (6.68m)
Machinery:	eight Thornycroft (Yarrow in Fiume) boilers driving two-shaft Parsons geared turbines, developing 95,000hp
Maximum speed:	32kt
Armour:	belt 5.9 to 4.72in (15 to 10cm); decks 2.75in to 0.78in (70mm to 20mm); bulkheads 4.7in to 3.5in (119mm to 89mm); main turrets 5.9in to 4.7in (150mm to 119mm)
Armament:	eight 8in (203mm) main guns, 16 4in (102mm) AA guns (later 14), six 40mm AA guns, eight 37mm AA guns, eight 13.2mm AA guns (later 16)
Complement:	841
Country:	Italy

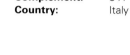

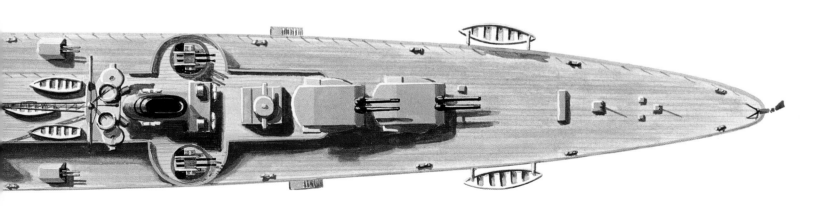

Prinz Eugen

By the mid-1930s, when the terms of the Washington Treaty had fallen into abeyance, Germany had already built six of the eight light cruisers permitted to it. The Anglo-German Naval Agreement that followed tried to rein in the development of the German fleet, but allowed the construction of five more 10,000-ton cruisers armed with 8in (203mm) guns. The Agreement blocked the building of these ships until January 1943, but as an interim step Germany would be allowed to launch a maximum of five 'treaty cruisers' armed with smaller 5.9in (149mm) guns. These ships were drawn up as what became the *Hipper* class, but when Russia announced that it intended to build seven cruisers with 7in (178mm) guns for the Baltic, the Germans immediately replaced their 5.9in (149mm) guns with 8in (203mm) guns. This is what the *Hipper* class became. They were not the equal of the earlier *Deutschland*s as they lacked their range and firepower, and some felt that they were not effective warships for the commerce raiding role that would be assigned to them. The five *Hipper*-class cruisers also had a sophisticated high-pressure steam propulsion system that demanded a very high level of training and operator expertise. *Prinz Eugen* was the first of the second batch of three *Hipper* cruisers to be laid down. However, the other two ships – *Seydlitz* and *Lützow* – were never completed as planned. This left *Prinz Eugen* partnered only with *Admiral Hipper* and *Blücher:* the latter was an early wartime loss, sunk during the Norwegian campaign. *Prinz Eugen* was laid down on 23 April 1936, launched on 22 August 1938 and commissioned on 1 August 1940. Together with the *Bismarck, Prinz Eugen* undertook the infamous 'channel dash' that took the two out into the North Atlantic. When *Bismarck* was sunk not long afterwards, *Prinz Eugen* managed to

evade the British fleet and find refuge in St Nazaire. The early, sizeable losses to Germany's major surface vessels caused Hitler to lose faith in that part of the navy. The remaining capital ships were pulled back into home waters and took little part in the rest of the war. *Prinz Eugen* was ceded to the US after the Potsdam Conference of 1945, and was used as a target ship in the Crossroads atomic tests at Bikini Atoll in July 1946. The German cruiser survived both the 'Able' air burst (which was dropped off target) and the far more devastating 'Baker' underwater shot three weeks later. *Prinz Eugen* remained afloat and was eventually towed away to sink off Kawajalein Atoll in August 1946.

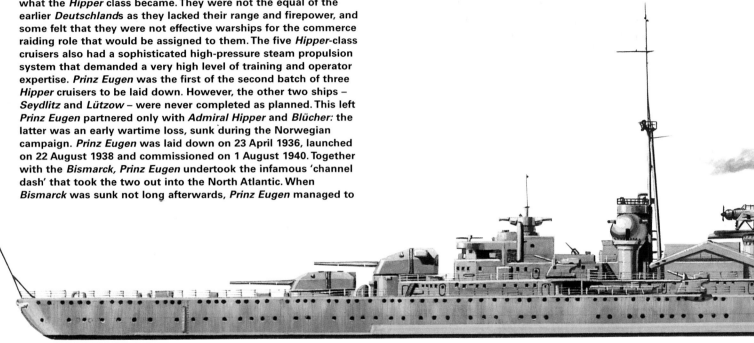

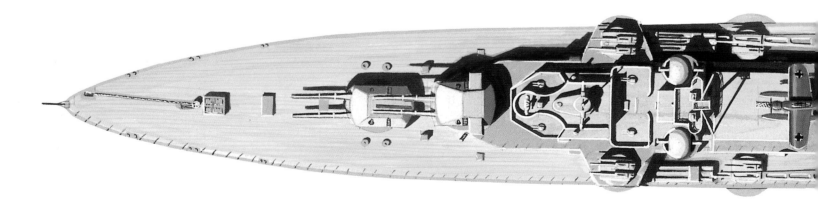

Cruisers

Specification

Displacement: 16,974t standard; 19,042t deep load
Dimensions: length (overall) 679ft 11.5in (207.25m); beam (at the waterline) 70ft 6in (21.48m); draught 23ft 7.5in (7.2m)
Machinery: nine Wagner (La Mont) boilers driving three-shaft Deschimag geared turbines, developing 132,000hp
Maximum speed: 32.5kt
Armour: belt 3.5in to 1.5in (89mm to 38mm); deck 1.5in to 1.25in (38mm to 31mm); torpedo bulkhead 0.75in (19mm); main turrets 6.25in to 2.25in (158mm to 57mm)
Armament: eight 8in (203mm) main guns, 12 4.1in (105mm) secondary guns, 12 37mm AA guns, eight 20mm AA guns, 12 21in (533mm) torpedo tubes, plus three aircraft
Complement: 1600
Country: Germany

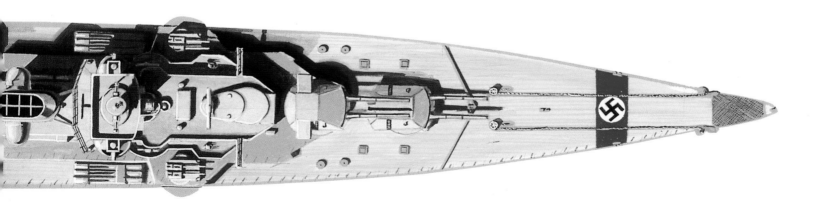

USS *Allen M. Sumner* (DD-692)

The lead ship in its class, the *Sumner* represented cutting-edge destroyer technology and 70 were built. The US ships were designed to counter the Japanese *Terutsuki*-class destroyers. The *Sumner* was laid down on 7 July 1943, launched on 15 December 1943 and commissioned on 26 January 1944. In October 1944 she sailed from Pearl Harbor for her first operational cruise. By November *Sumner* was supporting air strikes against the Philippines and arrived in the Leyte Gulf area in November. On 2 December 1944 she sailed with the destroyers USS *Cooper* and USS *Moale* to Ormac Bay where there had been reports of a Japanese convoy. Later that night the ships suffered the first of many aircraft attacks when a Mitsubishi Ki-46 dropped a bomb only yards from *Sumner* that started a fire on board. The US ships were next engaged by the Japanese destroyers *Kuwa* and *Take*: *Kuwa* was sunk by the combined force of the three

American vessels but then *Take* torpedoed and sank the *Cooper*. *Sumner* and *Moale* withdrew and survived, and *Sumner* went on to participate in the remaining Philippine campaigns. She was damaged in a kamikaze attack on 6 January 1945 but stayed on the line for several days until the situation allowed her to withdraw for repairs. *Sumner* saw out the rest of the war and was one of the escorts for the USS *Missouri* in the signing of the Japanese surrender. After 1945 USS *Sumner* still had a long operational career ahead of her as she supported the Crossroads atomic tests of 1946, took part in the Korean War, the Cuban missile crisis, the Dominican Republic crisis, the Gemini 10 space shot, the Vietnam war and a host of other duties. The *Sumner* was only retired from duty in 1973 but this historic ship was cut up for scrap in 1974.

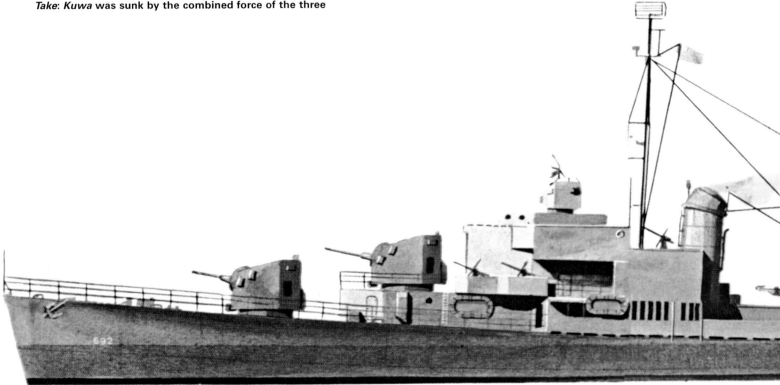

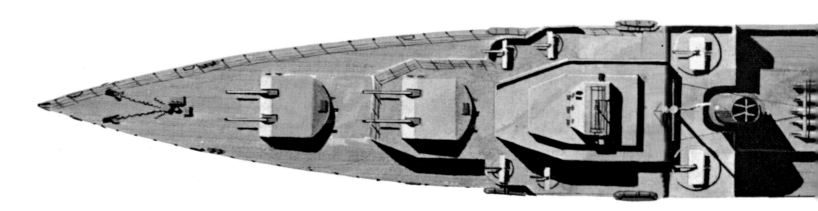

Destroyers

Specification

Displacement:	2610t standard; 3218t full load
Dimensions:	length (overall) 376ft 6in (114.68m); beam (at the waterline) 40ft 10in (12.44m); draught 14ft 2in (4.32m)
Machinery:	four Babcock & Wilcox boilers, driving two-shaft General Electric turbines, developing 60,000hp
Maximum speed:	36.5kt
Armour:	none
Armament:	six 5in (127mm) main guns, 12 40mm AA guns, 11 20mm AA guns, 10 21in (533mm) torpedo tubes
Complement:	336
Country:	USA

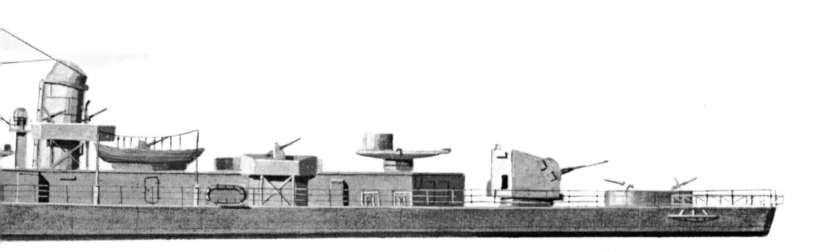

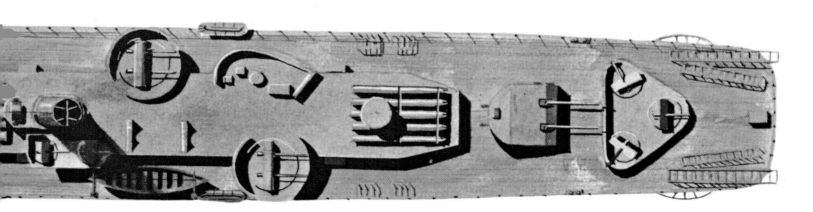

Karl Galster (Z20)

When Germany declared war the German navy had only a small force of 21 destroyers. Development of modern destroyer designs had begun in 1934, with the so-called 1934-type ships. All of Germany's pre-war destroyers were derived from this design. These ships were well-built and cleverly engineered but they were over-sophisticated, particularly in their powerplants, and technical troubles prevented them attaining their full design performance. Their designers only ever envisaged operations in the Baltic and North Seas, but in the event German destroyers operated around the entire coastline of occupied Europe. *Karl Galster* was one of the six 1936-type destroyers laid down between 1936 and 1937. She was launched on 15 June 1938. These vessels were similar to the improved 1934A type but had further augmented AA armament. By 1940, all German destroyers had been fitted with radar, but by April 1940 that force had been cut in half with the destruction of 10 destroyers by British forces in the Norwegian campaign. *Karl Galster* was the only one of its class to survive the war; the other five were sunk either at Narvik, or in Rombaksfjord. In 1946 the *Karl Galster* was handed over to the Soviet navy as part of Germany's war reparations to the Soviet Union. She served in the Baltic fleet as the *Protshnyi* into the 1950s.

Specification

Displacement:	1811t standard; 3415t full load
Dimensions:	length (overall) 410ft 1in (125m); beam (at the waterline) 38ft 8in (11.78m); draught 13ft 1in (3.98m)
Machinery:	six Wagner boilers, driving two-shaft Wagner geared turbines, developing 70,000hp
Maximum speed:	40kt
Armour:	none
Armament:	five 5in (127mm) main guns, four 37mm AA guns, seven 20mm AA guns, eight 21in (533mm) torpedo tubes
Complement:	315
Country:	Germany

HMS *Kelly*

Specification

Displacement:	2330t standard; 2540t full load
Dimensions:	length (overall) 356ft 6in (108.66m); beam (at the waterline) 35ft 8in (10.87m); draught 13ft 10in (4.22m)
Machinery:	two Admiralty three-drum boilers, driving two-shaft Parson geared turbines, developing 40,000hp
Maximum speed:	36kt
Armour:	none
Armament:	six 4.7in (119mm) main guns, four two-pounder 'pom pom' AA guns, 10 21in (533mm) torpedo tubes, 45 depth charges
Complement:	183 to 218
Country:	GB

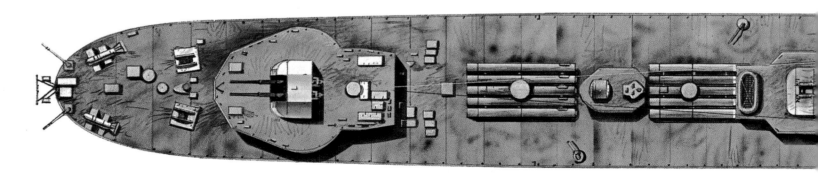

Destroyers

From 1929 onwards the Royal Navy took to giving its destroyer classes letter names, which corresponded with the individual ship's names. Under this system, the *C* class included HMS *Comet* and HMS *Crescent*, while the *D* class included HMS *Duncan* and HMS *Dainty*. HMS *Kelly* was the lead ship of the *K* class, which was built alongside the *J* and *N* class destroyers. The *J* and *K* class ships were laid down between 1937 and 1938 and HMS *Kelly* herself was launched on 25 October 1938. These destroyers were the first such British design to feature a single funnel since HMS *Fervent* and HMS *Zephyr* of 1895. The *K* class drew on the experience of the preceding *Tribal*-class ships (a joint British-Canadian destroyer series that bucked the trend for letter names). The *Tribal*s were heavy destroyers, intended to take on rival ships such as Japan's *Fubuki* class. The *K* class featured the same 4.7in (119mm) guns as the *Tribal* destroyers, and were also armed with torpedoes and depth charges. By the end of the war the surviving ships had been upgunned with additional 20mm and 40mm AA guns. In all eight *K*-class destroyers were built between 1938 and 1939. Of these, four were lost to enemy action and one was destroyed by an accidental internal explosion. HMS *Kelly* was one of the unlucky ships. Famed as the flagship of Lord Louis Mountbatten's flotilla, the *Kelly* was heavily engaged in the ill-fated British defence of Crete. On 20 May 1941, the *Kelly* and her unit came under persistent Stuka attack. While making 30kt and turning hard to port, the vessel suffered severe bomb damage. Still moving fast, HMS *Kelly* rolled over and capsized, sinking in half an hour. The survivors had to endure continuing air attack.

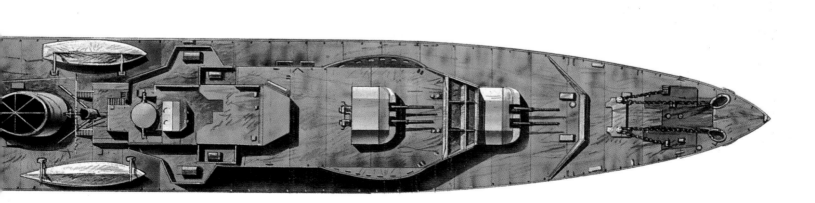

USS *Johnston* (DD-557)

The *Fletcher*-class destroyers were by far the largest class of US destroyers, with over 300 vessels built. The *Fletcher*s were the first US destroyers to be built (essentially) free of treaty restrictions in the 1930s and so they became larger and better armed than previous ships. They featured a flush-deck hull which reduced interior space but to their crews, the *Fletcher*s were the epitome of destroyer design and superior to the *Sumner* class that followed. Several experimental changes were made to some *Fletcher*s, including new powerplants, and three were fitted with catapults to carry aircraft. At least one vessel saw combat in this configuration, but it ultimately proved to be a disappointment. The USS *Johnston* was laid down on 6 May 1942, launched on 25 March 1943 and commissioned on 27 October 1943. Three months later she was engaged in the Marshall Islands and Solomons campaign, shelling the beaches at Kwajalein, Eniwetok, Kapingamarangi Atoll and Empress Agusta Bay. On 25 May 1944 she depth-charged and sank the Japanese submarine *I-16*. *Johnston* partnered the battleship *Pennsylvania* in the Guam bombardment and supported the Palau invasions in July/August. However, *Johnston*'s place in history was to come in the recapture of the Philippines in October 1944. On 23 October 1944 the Japanese and American fleets fired the opening shots in what would become known as the Battle of Leyte Gulf. Acting as part of Carrier Task Group 774 the USS *Johnston* found itself confronting the Japanese Centre Force, which had slipped past the rest of the US fleet. A handful of US destroyers was all that stood between the unprotected US carrier force and four Japanese battleships, seven cruisers and at least 12 destroyers. The US ships began to lay down smoke and zig-zag. It took 20 minutes for the Japanese force to come within range of the *Johnston*'s 5in (127mm) guns, but when it could the destroyer engaged and badly damaged the cruiser *Kumano*. *Johnston* was then hit by three 14in (356mm) shells followed by three 6in (152mm) shells; she lost power and her own guns were badly damaged. With power restored *Johnston* returned to the battle and in the smoke and confusion nearly collided with another US destroyer. She attacked a battleship and engaged a Japanese destroyer squadron, fighting it to a standstill. More shells fell upon the *Johnston* as she fought to protect the five American carriers being hunted by the Japanese ships. Finally the destroyer lost all power as the one remaining engine room was knocked out, and on 24 October 1944 the USS *Johnston* was abandoned and sank. Of the 327 crew on board only 141 were saved. For supreme courage and daring in the Battle of Samar, the ship and her crew were awarded a Presidential Unit Citation.

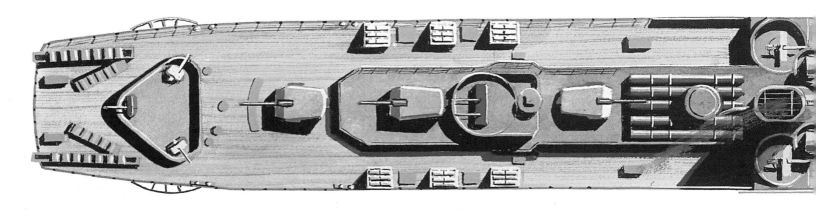

Destroyers

Specification

Displacement: 2325t standard; 2924t full load
Dimensions: length (overall) 376ft 5in (114.73m); beam (at the waterline) 39ft 7in (12.06m); draught 13ft 9in (4.19m)
Machinery: four Babcock & Wilcox boilers, driving two-shaft General Electric turbines, developing 60,000hp
Maximum speed: 38kt
Armour: side 0.75in (19mm); deck over machinery 0.5in (12mm)
Armament: five 5in (127mm) main guns, four 28mm guns, four 20mm AA guns, 10 21in (533mm) torpedo tubes
Complement: 273
Country: USA

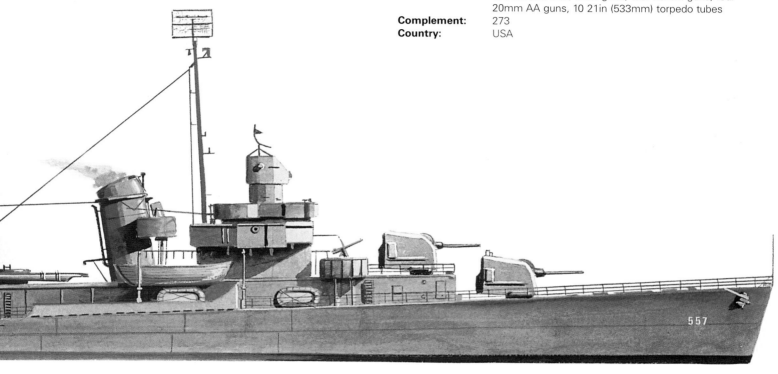

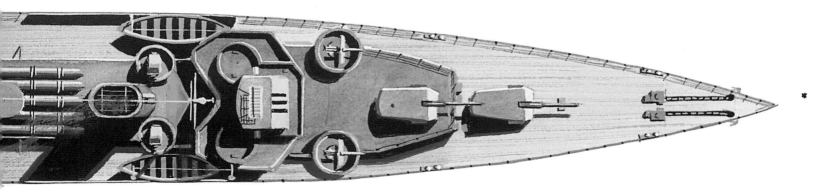

Yukikaze

The *Kagero*-class destroyers were the most modern of their type available to the Japanese navy when war broke out in Europe. They were similar to the earlier *Asashio* class, but could take advantage of a refined design that had been well and truly 'wrung out'. They were also noteworthy for their high speed, a general feature of all Japanese destroyers. The lead ship in the class, *Kagero*, was launched in September 1938. *Yukikaze* was the sixth *Kagero* destroyer and was launched at the Sasebo naval yard on 24 March 1939. All 18 vessels were in service by early 1941. The *Kageros* were designed with three twin 5in (127mm) gun turrets but the centre X turret was deleted from the remaining ships between 1943 and 1944 to make way for more

AA armament. This, in turn, was increased continuously during the war until, by June 1944, some destroyers were carrying 24 25mm cannon and four 13.2mm guns. One of the *Kagero* class, *Hamakaze*, made a small contribution to Japanese naval history by becoming the first Japanese destroyer to be fitted with radar. The smaller combat vessels of the Japanese fleet were virtually wiped out by the US Navy and the *Kagero* class was no exception, although it was virtually the only Japanese destroyer class not to have every member sunk by 1945. Of the 18 ships built only *Yukikaze* survived the war, one of half a dozen destroyers to survive from a total force of over 100 vessels.

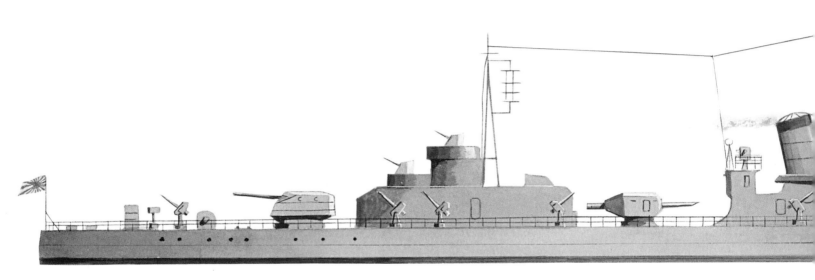

Destroyers

Specification

Displacement: 2033t standard; 2450t trial
Dimensions: length (overall) 388ft 9in (118.49m); beam (at the waterline) 35ft 5in (10.79m); draught 12ft 4in (3.76m)
Machinery: three boilers driving two-shaft geared turbines, developing 52,000hp
Maximum speed: 35kt
Armour: none
Armament: six 5in (127mm) main guns, four 25mm AA guns, eight 24in (609mm) torpedo tubes, 16 depth charges
Complement: 240
Country: Japan

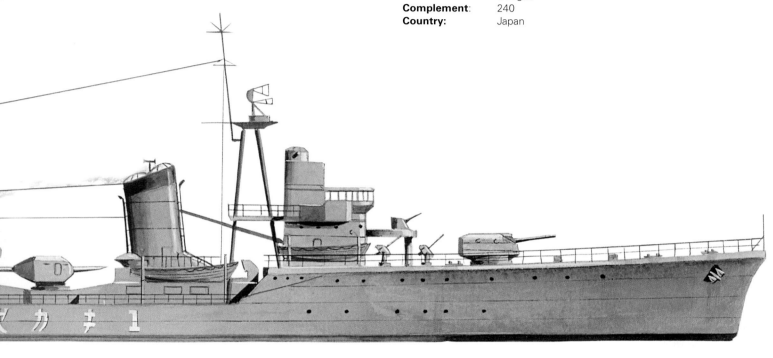

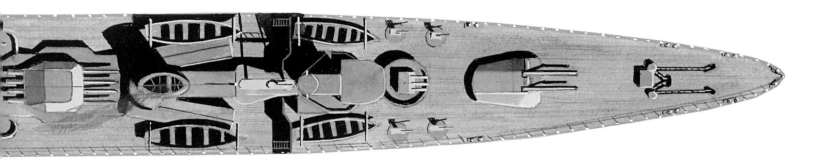

I-400

Japan did not use its submarines wisely during World War II. Japanese naval strategy was drawn towards grand and decisive engagements – like Pearl Harbor – and the covert nature of submarine warfare did not seem to serve this goal. By 1941 Japan had built up a large and varied submarine fleet and continued to build new boats throughout the war. However, despite a handful of notable successes, the Japanese submarine fleet failed to make any sizeable impact on the conduct of the war, unlike the American submarines. Japanese submarines were hardly ever used to attack US supply ships in the Pacific but instead were deployed against the ever-more deadly surface battle groups. This lack of understanding also permeated Japan's merchant fleet: in general, cargo ships were never convoyed but left to fend for themselves, becoming easy pickings for the US submarines. Perhaps the best evidence of the Japanese naval planners' failure to understand the role of the submarine can be found in the *STO* class, of which submarine *I-400* was the first. These vessels were also known as the *Sen Toku*, or *Toku Gata Sensuikan* – literally special class submarine. The *STO*-class was an aircraft-carrying submarine, drawn up as part of a futile plan to launch air raids on the Panama Canal. A special type of aircraft, the Aichi M6AI Seiran (meaning clear sky storm) was developed for the *Sen Tokus*. The *STO*s were the largest

submarines to be built during World War II and they were intended to operate in conjunction with the smaller *AM* class which would carry scouting aircraft for the *STO*s bombers. The *STO*-class had a single hangar, located below and to starboard of the conning tower, which was offset to port. A single catapult was fitted and up to three aircraft could be carried. The practicalities of such a vessel surfacing, opening huge watertight doors, launching aircraft and submerging again – let alone recovering the aircraft later – hardly bear thinking about, but it was accomplished successfully in training. *I-400* had an astonishing design range of 30,000nm (55,560km), but it never made it into the war. *I-400*, *I-401* and *I-402* were launched between 1944 and 1945, but *I-402* was converted to act as a submarine fuel tanker. *I-400* and *I-401* prepared for their intended Panama Canal attack but in the last days of the war they were redirected to attack the US invasion fleet, which was believed to be massing off the Japanese coast. On 16 August 1945 the two submarines, still en route to their targets, were recalled after Japan surrendered. The other *STO*-class boats once on order had all been cancelled and, while it is possible that some were partially built, they were all destroyed in air raids on the Kure naval yard in 1945. *I-400* and *I-401* were used as gunnery targets after the war in 1946.

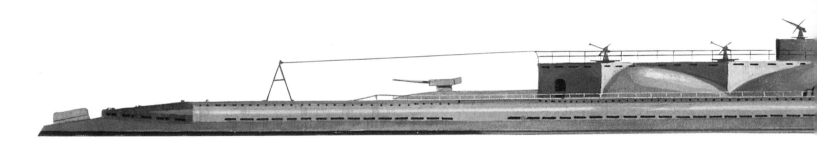

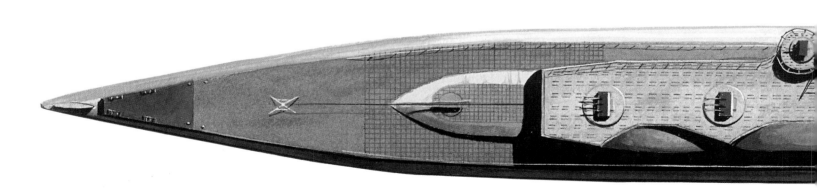

Specification

Displacement:	3530t standard; 6560t submerged
Dimensions:	length (overall) 400ft 3in (122m); beam (at the waterline) 39ft 4in (11.98m); draught 23ft (7m)
Machinery:	two-shaft diesel electrics plus electric motors, developing 7700hp
Maximum speed:	18.7kt (6.5kt submerged)
Armour:	none
Armament:	eight 21in (533mm) torpedo tubes, one 5.5in (140mm) main gun, 10 25mm AA guns, plus three aircraft
Complement:	80
Country:	Japan

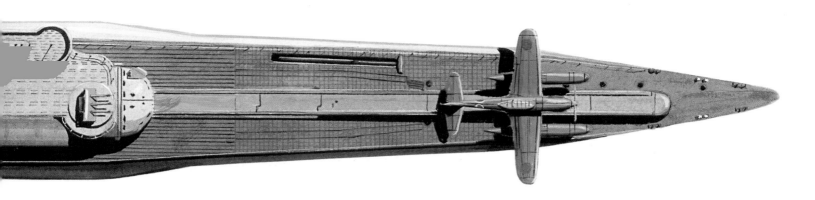

USS *Ray* (SS-271)

During World War II the United States developed several classes of 'fleet submarines' that were different to those in service with other nations. Whereas German submarines, for example, were optimised to cruise on the surface and only submerge when attacking their targets, US submarines were better suited to long-range underwater cruising. This approach was driven by the need to have submarines operating far out in the Pacific – not only attacking Japanese shipping but also gathering intelligence. Until the late 1930s the US submarine fleet was modest and it was not until the outbreak of war in the Pacific that the fleet was expanded in any meaningful way. However, once the US Navy found itself at war the submarine fleet grew at an astonishing rate. Three classes of fleet submarine shouldered the load during World War II; the *Gato*-, *Balao*- and *Tench*-class boats. Over 300 were built and by the end of the war these submarines had an operational range of 11,000nm (20,372km) while carrying 28 torpedoes. The USS *Ray* was one of the late-build *Gato*-class submarines, laid down on 20 July 1942, launched on 28 February 1943 and commissioned on 27

July 1943. These boats were originally fitted with a single 3in (76mm) deck gun, aft of the conning tower, but by the end of the war, two 5in (127mm) guns had been installed instead. As with other vessels, armament configurations varied widely and many submarines were fitted with light 20mm and 40mm AA guns. During her first war patrol in November 1943, *Ray* was deployed to the Bismarck Archipelago where she attacked a Japanese convoy, sinking a freighter and a gunboat. *Ray* made a total of eight war patrols, sinking 32 Japanese ships (including 16 small craft destroyed by gunfire in one engagement) across the Pacific – this total does not include the many damaged vessels and unconfirmed kills. *Ray* had several close calls in Japanese counter-attacks and was damaged on a few occasions. In 1944 the submarine was nearly lost when she crash-dived to escape an enemy aircraft, but with an unsecured conning tower hatch. *Ray* was flooded but kept under control and returned to Mios Woendi for repairs. The USS *Ray* served long after the end of World War II, like many of its sister-ships, and was only withdrawn in 1958. She was scrapped in 1960.

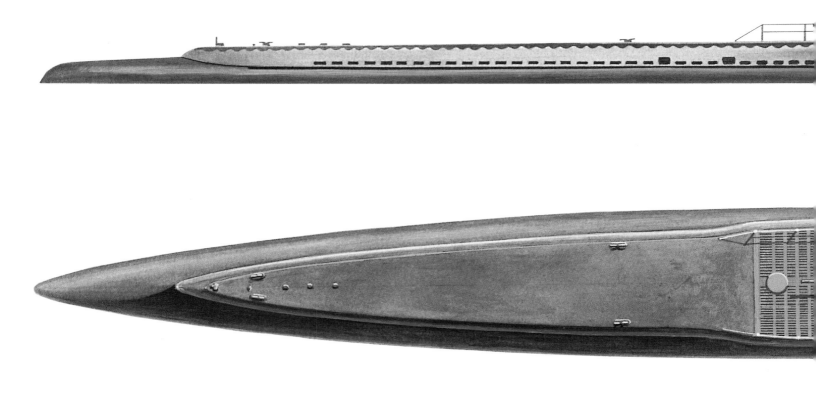

Specification

Displacement: 1526t standard; 2410t submerged
Dimensions: length (overall) 311ft 9in (95m); beam (at the waterline) 27ft 3in (8.3m); draught 15ft 3in (4.64m)
Machinery: two-shaft diesel electrics plus electric motors, developing 5400hp
Maximum speed: 20.25kt (8.75kt submerged)
Armour: none
Armament: 10 21in (533mm) torpedo tubes (six bow, four stern), one 3in (76mm) main gun, two 12.7mm machine guns, two 7mm machine guns (standard)
Complement: 80
Country: USA

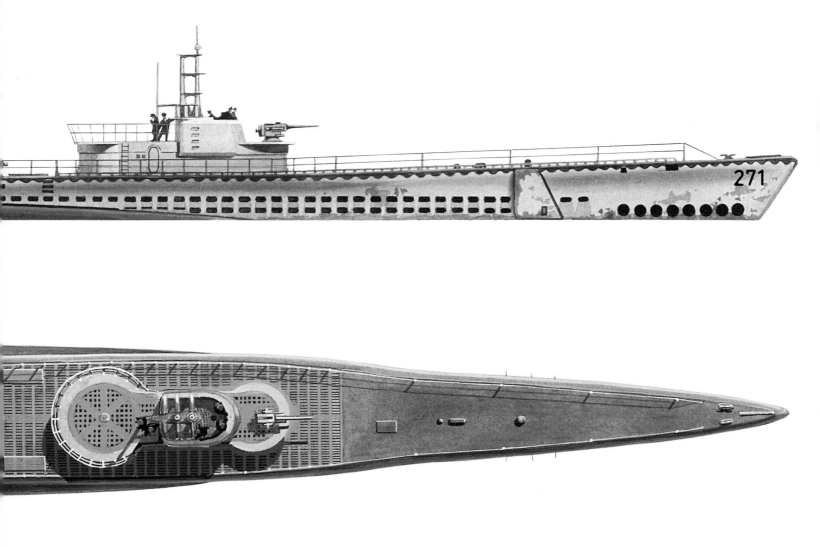

USS *Tench* (SS-417)

The USS *Tench* was the lead boat in the *Tench*-class, the ultimate evolution of the US wartime 'fleet' submarine. She was laid down on 1 April 1944 and launched on 7 July 1944. While her design clearly shows the heritage of the preceding *Gato*- and *Balao*-class boats, the *Tench* was a more sophisticated submarine. About 30 of this class were built before the war ended. Despite their excellent basic engineering it was not until late 1943 that the US submarine fleet became truly effective. Before then, submarine operations were hampered by very poor torpedo design, which led to the weapons misfiring or failing to explode on a regular basis. It took years to solve this problem, but once remedied the US attack submarines became so successful that follow-on orders were cancelled because the existing force had virtually run out of Japanese targets. The weapons fit changed throughout the war as heavy calibre guns were replaced by lighter but faster firing weapons, chiefly for AA protection. These were fitted on the 'cigarette deck', on either

side of the conning tower. Some submarines were even fitted with rockets for shore bombardments. *Tench* joined a submarine attack group in February 1945 and was deployed off the Japanese coast on weather patrol, reconnaissance and life guard duties. After an unconfirmed sinking of a large Japanese vessel in April, *Tench* was redeployed as part of the picket line of submarines blocking the approaches to Okinawa, but was not involved in the sinking of the *Yamato*. During her second war patrol in May, *Tench* sank two Japanese merchantmen, a tanker and a motor trawler, and damaged a destroyer. During her final cruise she was attacked by two Japanese bombers but escaped, and survived the war unscathed. The USS *Tench* and her sister-ships went on to form the backbone of the US submarine fleet until the early 1960s and surplus boats were exported to navies around the world. *Tench* was converted to a *Guppy* 1A class and remained operational until 1969. She was sold to Peru in 1976, and used for spares.

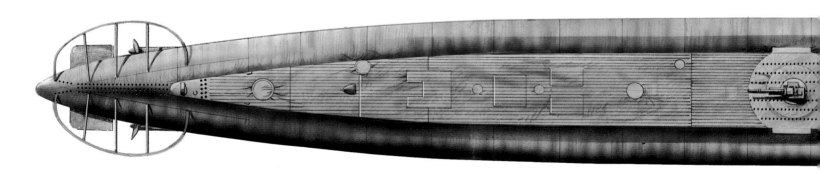

Submarines

Specification

Displacement: 1570t standard; 2415t submerged
Dimensions: length (overall) 311ft 8in (94.9m); beam (at the waterline) 27ft 3in (8.3m); draught 15ft 5in (4.7m)
Machinery: two-shaft diesel electrics plus electric motors, developing 5400hp
Maximum speed: 20.25kt (8.75kt submerged)
Armour: none
Armament: 10 21in (533mm) torpedo tubes (six bow, four stern), one 3in (76mm) main gun, two 12.6mm machine guns, two 7mm machine guns (standard)
Complement: 80
Country: USA

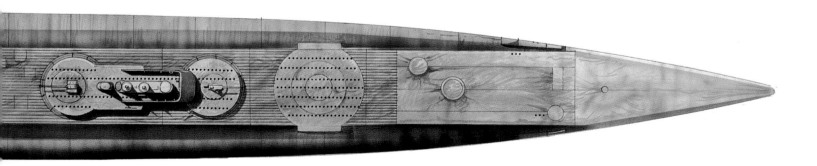

U-47

Germany knew that its U-boat fleet had nearly brought Britain to its knees during World War I – and the Allies knew it all too well too. The Treaty of Versailles specifically prohibited any German submarine operations or development, but this was circumvented by the foundation of a secret design bureau in Holland. Once Hitler had seized power and begun to flout the Versailles terms, the know-how to rebuild the German submarine fleet was ready and waiting. By 1934, designs for the ocean-going Type VII submarines had been drawn up, and these boats would become the backbone of Germany's submarine fleet throughout the war. It was Type VIIs that formed the 'wolfpacks', attacked the Atlantic convoys and nearly defeated Britain for a second time. Several versions of the Type VII were developed, of which the most significant was the Type VIIC, backing up the very similar Type VIIB. *U-47* was an early Type VIIB submarine, of which 24 were built (over 600 Type VIICs were built). *U-47* was also the submarine commanded by Lt Cmdr Gunther Prien which, in 1939, sunk the battleship HMS *Royal Oak*, inside Scapa Flow, one of the most daring submarine attacks of the war and a bitter blow to British prestige. Prien became the Kriegsmarine's first U-boat

'ace', and for his audacious raid he was awarded the Knight's Cross by the Führer himself. The Type VIIBs were built in the Germaniawerft, Vulcan and Flenderwerft shipyards between 1938 and 1941. As German submarine technology progressed, changes were made to the surviving Type VIIBs, including the addition of radar, the schnorkel system and new 37mm guns replacing the 3.4in (88mm) guns. However, by 1943 the existing classes of U-boat were being dominated by the Allies' superior anti-submarine warfare tactics. Even though Germany had developed some highly sophisticated new technology for its submarines – including streamlined hulls and air-independent propulsion (even now still thought of as futuristic) – none of these technologies had been incorporated into production designs. By the time their importance was understood it was too late and Germany continued to build obsolete Type VIIs until 1945. The German U-boat arm commissioned a total of 1170 submarines during World War II. Of these 630 boats were sunk, 42 lost in accidents, 81 were lost in harbour air raids, 38 were damaged beyond repair, 11 were interned in neutral countries and 215 were scuttled at the end of the war. Of the Type VIIBs all but four were sunk, including *U-47*.

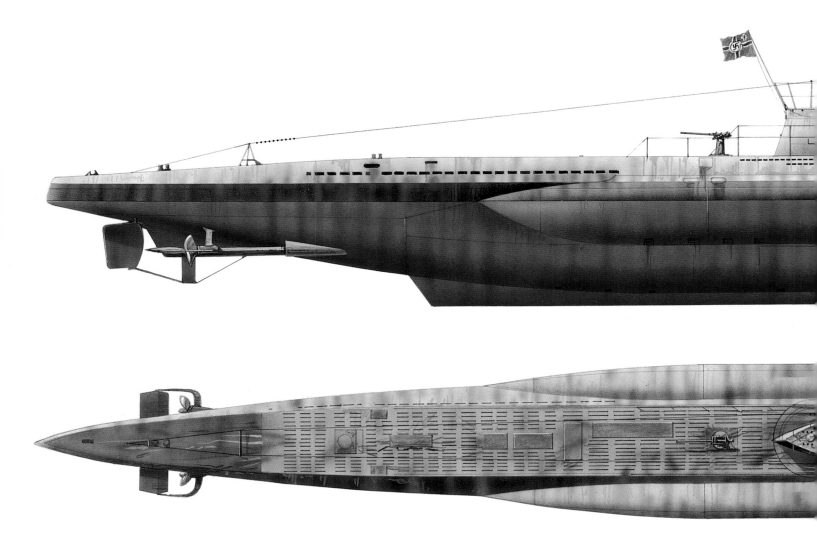

Specification

Displacement:	741t standard; 843t submerged
Dimensions:	length (overall) 218ft 2in (66.5m); beam (at the waterline) 24ft 4in (7.4m); draught 15ft 5in (4.7m)
Machinery:	two shafts, two diesels plus electric motors, developing 1400hp
Maximum speed:	17.2kt (8.8kt submerged)
Armour:	none
Armament:	five 21in (533mm) torpedo tubes (four bow, one stern) with 14 torpedoes, one 3.4in (88mm) main gun, one 20mm AA gun (standard)
Complement:	44
Country:	Germany

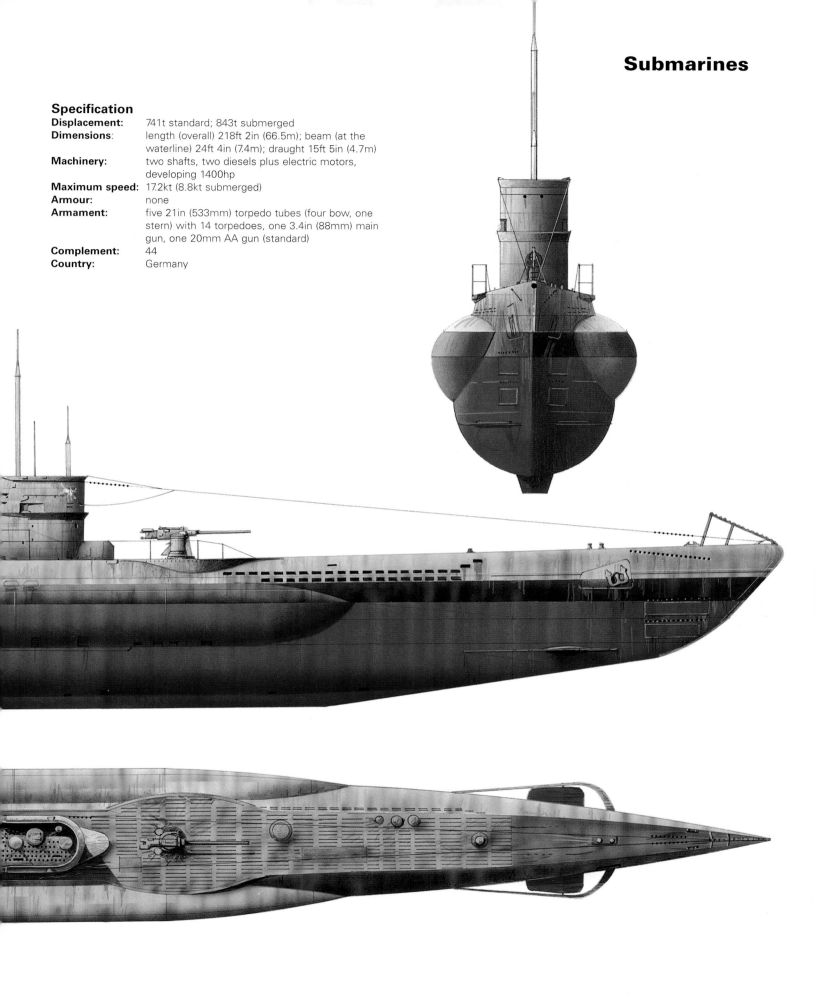

LST

The standard US tank landing craft (LST), which has now become an almost timeless design, grew from a British requirement for a tank carrier capable of transporting new tanks from US factories directly to Europe. What emerged as the LST had to be able to carry about 20 tanks, or equivalent vehicles, which could be driven straight off the ship via a ramp in the bow. Some tanks could be carried on the weather deck, above the main hold, and so the early LSTs had a lift between the two decks (this was later replaced by a ramp). The LSTs were also required to carry at least one tank landing craft (LCT) to allow operations in waters where the larger LST could not make it to the beach. The LSTs were designed to have great range, up to and beyond 5000nm (9260km). They were also very slow and could manage only about 10 kt when loaded and underway. This left them vulnerable to enemy fire and it was not for nothing that they were nicknamed

'Large Slow Targets'. To support the recapture of the Pacific Islands the US built a huge number of LSTs, 1152 in all. With Britain crying out for similar ships, many LSTs were transferred to the Royal Navy where they were known as LST Mk IIs or LST(2)s, though Britain also developed its own LST designs. The US-built ships proved highly successful and some survive in use with smaller navies even today. Alongside the tanks the LSTs could also carry up to 163 troops. Differences between individual LSTs could be substantial, with several davit configurations and a wide range of armament fits. By the end of the war, most US LSTs were fitted with seven 40mm and 12 20mm AA guns, but there were many exceptions to this rule. The hull design proved to be highly versatile and LSTs were converted to serve as MTB tenders, aircraft engine repair ships, salvage craft tenders, battle-damage repair ships and auxiliaries.

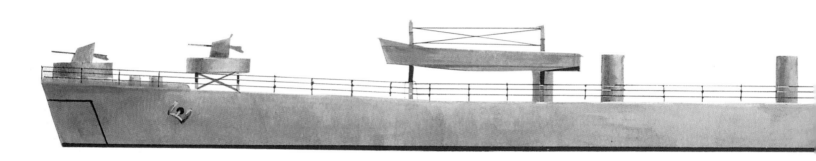

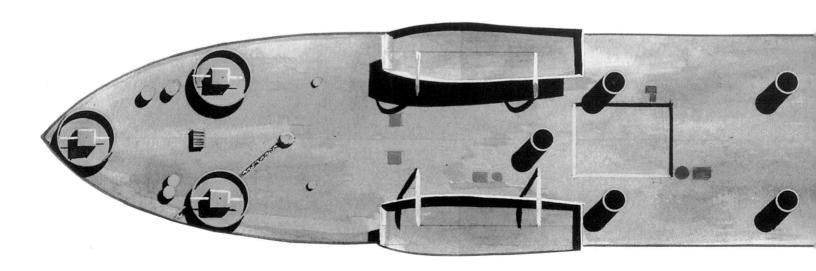

Landing Ships

Specification

Displacement:	1625t light; 2366t beaching; 4080t deep load
Dimensions:	length (overall) 328ft (99.9m); beam (at the waterline) 50ft (15.24m); draught 9ft 10in (2.99m)
Machinery:	two-shaft diesel engine, developing 1800hp
Maximum speed:	12kt
Armour:	none
Armament:	seven 40mm Bofors AA guns, 12 20mm AA guns
Complement:	111
Country:	USA

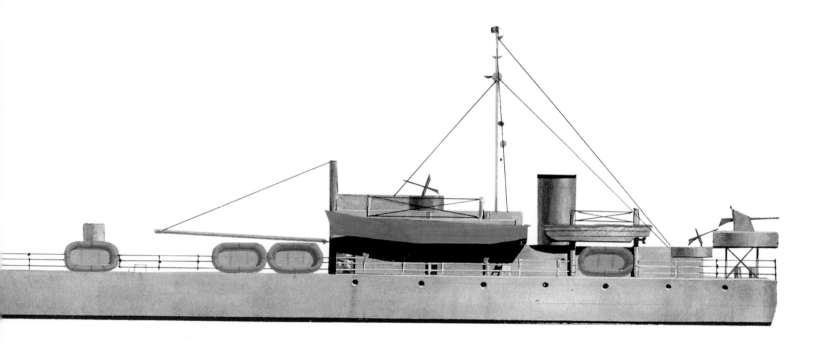

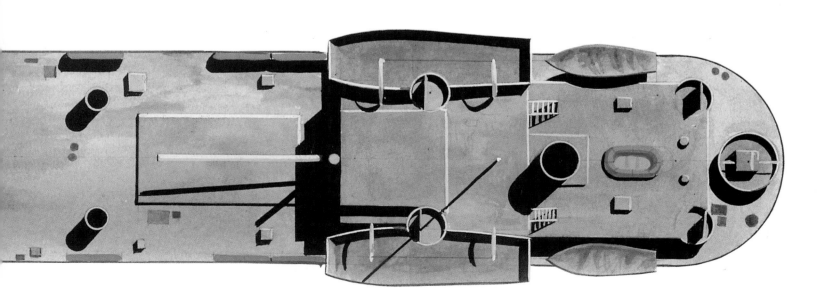

LST Mk 3

Britain built its own range of specialist amphibious warfare ships, large and small, including tank landing ships (LSTs). US-built LSTs served alongside British LSTs, and the American vessels were known as LST Mk IIs or LST(2)s. However, all LSTs had British design roots which could be traced back to the LST Mk I or LST(1). The LST(2) was a compromise between the sea-going qualities of the first British-designed tank landing ships, and the simplicity and ease of construction that came with the larger landing craft then being built. The LST(2) proved to be a successful design but there were simply not enough of them available to meet British and US demands in the later years of

the war. To remedy this the UK developed another class of LST, the LST Mk III or LST(3). These had roughly the same dimensions as the US LSTs, but were much heavier (due to their diesel engines and riveted construction) and thus more powerful. The LST(3)s were all launched between 1944 and 1945. A total of 62 were built in US and Canadian yards. More were ordered but some hulls were diverted to become merchant ships and others were cancelled at the end of the war. The ships could carry 15 40-ton tanks or 20 25-ton tanks, plus 14 3-ton trucks and up to 170 troops. The LST(3)s proved to be remarkably versatile and after the war most remained in service even into the 1970s.

Landing Ships

Specification

Displacement: 2300t standard; 4980t deep load
Dimensions: length (overall) 347ft 6in (105.8m); beam (at the waterline) 55ft 3in (16.84m); draught 12ft 5in (3.78m)
Machinery: two Admiralty three-drum boilers with two-shaft VTE, developing 5500hp
Maximum speed: 13.5kt
Armour: none
Armament: four 40mm Bofors AA guns, six 20mm AA guns (or 10 20mm only)
Complement: 118 to 190
Country: GB

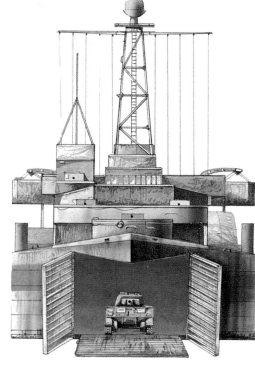

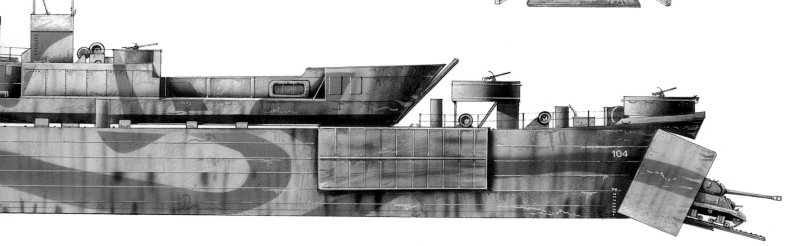

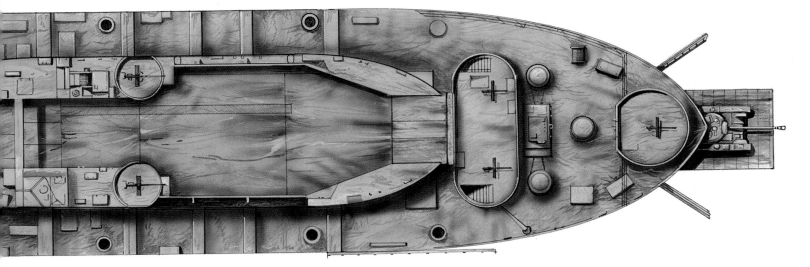

HMS *Anchusa*

The bulk of convoy escort duties were handled by corvettes from the Royal Navy and the Royal Canadian Navy. In turn, the bulk of the corvettes were the *Flower*-class or modified *Flower*-class ships, which played one of the most important and unsung roles of the entire war at sea. Over 200 *Flower*-class ships were built. The class was based on a pre-war whaler design drawn up by Smith's Docks, which was lengthened by about 30ft (9.14m) and fitted out with military equipment. They were built in 30 different ship yards in the UK and Canada, with the highest number being produced by Belfast's Harland & Wolff. HMS *Anchusa* was one of the 34 *Flower*-class ships built in Northern Ireland, which were launched between 1940 and 1942. There were differences, large and small, across the fleet, especially in armament. By the end of

the war the weapons fit on most of the *Flower*s had changed at least once, though most ships kept the 4in (102mm) main gun. The role of the corvette was to escort merchant shipping in convoy, and if possible, to find and attack enemy submarines. Their chief weapon was the Hedgehog anti-submarine mortar. Hedgehog consisted of high-explosive rockets fired in groups which would (hopefully) straddle the target U-boat and force it to the surface. In practice the 35lb (16kg) Torpex warheads carried by the rockets needed to score a direct hit to achieve any effect and Hedgehog was most useful in shallow waters. Standard depth charges were also carried. A total of 34 *Flower*-class ships were lost during the course of the war, but *Anchusa* survived the conflict.

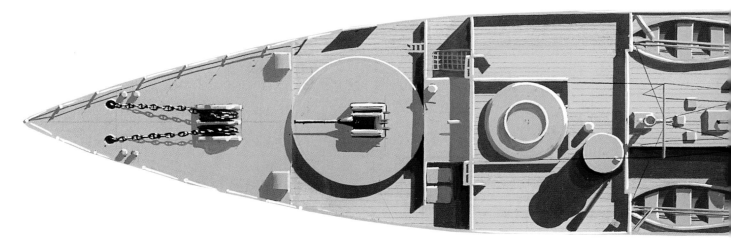

Specification

Displacement:	1170t standard; 1390t deep load
Dimensions:	length (overall) 205ft (62.48m); beam (at the waterline) 33ft 2in (10.1m); draught 15ft 9in (4.8m)
Machinery:	two boilers, driving one-shaft VTE, developing 2750hp
Maximum speed:	16.5kt
Armour:	none
Armament:	one 4in (102mm) main gun, 40 depth charges, 72 Hedgehog rockets
Complement:	85 to 109
Country:	GB

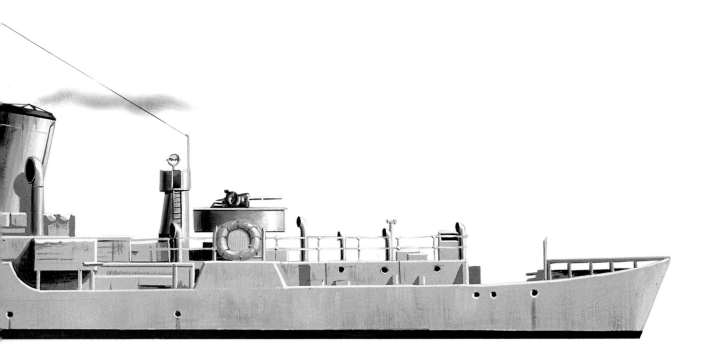

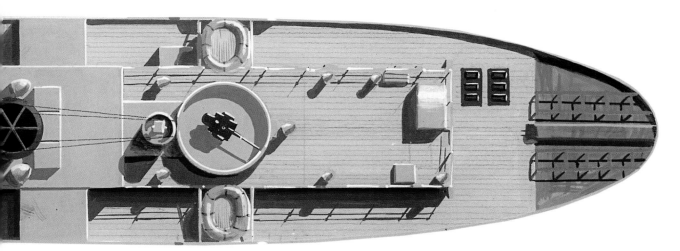

Fairmile Type C MTB

Britain developed a range of motor torpedo-boats (MTBs), motor gun boats (MGBs) and motor anti-submarine boats (MA/SBs) to serve with the coastal forces. All eventually became grouped under the MTB classification. Their role was to harry enemy shipping and guard against intruders. They were also tasked with specialist roles such as inserting Commando teams, minelaying/minesweeping and providing fast targets for other units. MTBs were built in large numbers,

by a range of shipyards such as Vosper, Whites, Camper & Nicholson, British Power Boats and Thornycroft, and to a range of different designs. The Fairmile series of MTBs were developed from the earlier Type A and Type B motor launches/minelayers, which led to the Type C and larger Type D MTBs. This vessel is a Type C MTB, known individually by their pennant numbers (MGB312-335). The first Type C was launched in 1941 and of the 23 built, five were lost during the war.

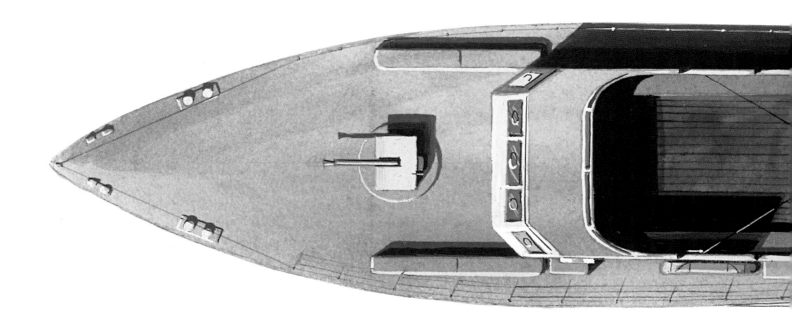

Escorts and Patrol Ships

Specification

Displacement: 69t standard; 75t deep load
Dimensions: length (overall) 117ft (35.66m); beam (at the waterline) 17ft 5in (5.3m); draught 5ft 8in (1.73m)
Machinery: three-shaft Hall-Scott petrol engines, developing 2700hp
Maximum speed: 27kt
Armour: none
Armament: two two-pounder 'pom pom' AA guns, four 12.6mm machine guns, four 7.6mm machine guns (later six 20mm and four 7.6mm guns)
Complement: 16
Country: GB

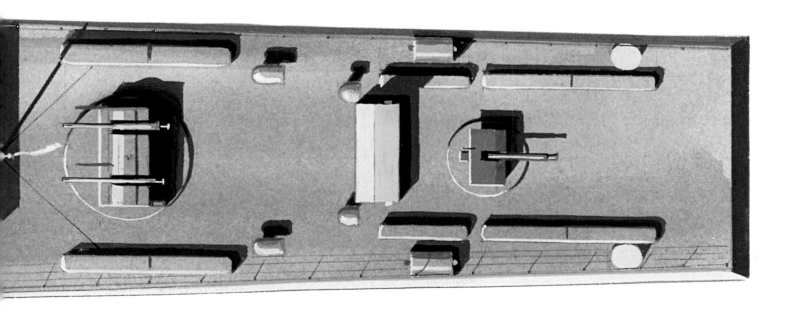

HMS *Jervis Bay*

As the war in Europe worsened, Britain became totally
dependent on the Atlantic convoys to bring essential supplies
from the United States. Once Britain stood alone against Hitler's
war machine, her fate would be decided on whether or not the
convoys could get through. However, the convoys were tempting
targets for German submarines or surface raiders, and there
simply were not enough front-line naval vessels available to
escort them. To provide a modicum of protection, chiefly against
U-boats running on the surface (gun attacks were then an
effective U-boat tactic) Britain adapted commercial shipping to
serve as armed merchant cruisers. HMS *Jervis Bay* was one of
over 50 such vessels commissioned between 1939 and 1940.
Jervis Bay was a 1922-vintage ship of 14,000 tons, and a former
passenger liner. Like most of her fellow armed merchant cruisers
she was fitted with old Mk VII 6in (152mm) guns, which did not
use high velocity charges. As a result the guns had a very limited
range. Attempts were made to improve this situation on other
ships in later years, and AA armament was also improved in
several cases. Between 1939 and 1942, 14 armed merchant
cruisers were lost, while those that survived generally went on to
serve as troopships in the later stages of the war. HMS *Jervis Bay*
was one of the unlucky ones. She was sunk by the *Admiral
Scheer* on 5 November 1940.

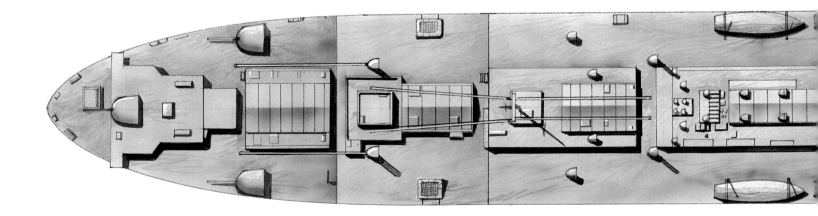

Specification

Displacement:	14,164t
Dimensions:	unavailable
Machinery:	unavailable
Maximum speed:	15kt
Armour:	none
Armament:	seven 6in (152mm) guns
Complement:	unavailable
Country:	GB

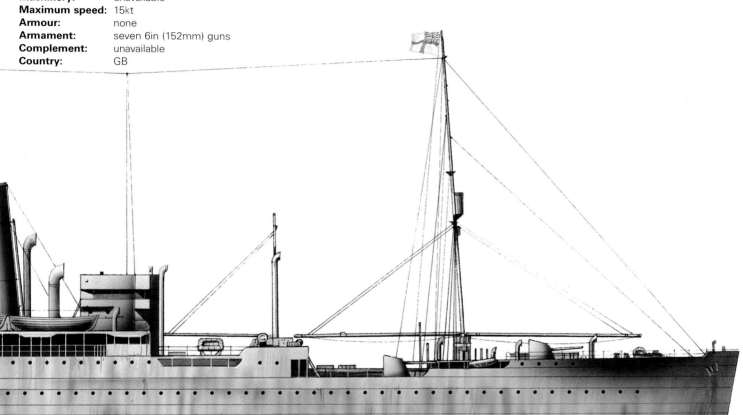

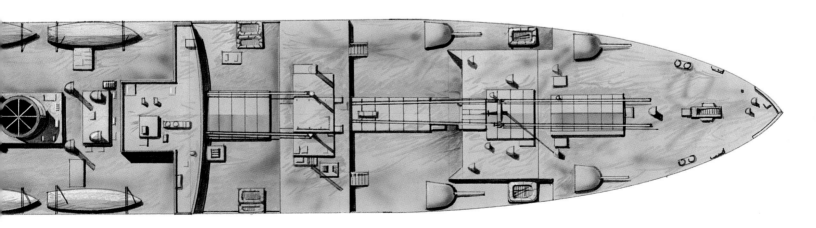